Table Of Contents

Dedication And Acknowledgements 4

Foreword 5

Chapter 1: The VAK Model (Video-Audio-Kinesthetic) 6

Chapter 2: Motivation 17

Chapter 3: Drummer Self-Esteem 35

Chapter 4: Setting Goals 43

Chapter 5: Conflict 51

Chapter 6: Anxiety, Fear, And Stress 60

Chapter 7: Band Dynamics 76

Chapter 8: Mind Matters 82

Chapter 9: One-Shots 113

About The Author 120

Dedication And Acknowledgements

This work is respectfully dedicated to
Drs. Carmen Giuliano and Lawrence E. White.

~good doctors ~good men

Without you two, I never would have made it through the
last four years.

Special thanks to: Michael Dawson, my editor, drum mentor, and good friend; Walfredo Reyes Jr., my close friend
and drum sensei; my mom and my brother, Mike, my
greatest literary supporters, my gentlest critics; Alta,
Nikki, and Karla; all the editors and staff at *Modern
Drummer*; and all my drum brothers and sisters who, after
hearing a stick rebound off a stretched skin, felt that primal resonance deep within.

Foreword

When we were born, it would have been very helpful if someone had given us a user's manual for our mind. No such luck. So as we grew up, we made our way in the world with the help of our parents, teachers, and friends, plus the aid of our own instinctual coping mechanisms. What we learned, however, was often biased, tainted, and sometimes just downright wrong. We often internalized some very irrational and erroneous thoughts and beliefs. The offshoot of these beliefs is that they made—and sometimes continue to make—existence in our own skin quite difficult. These negative thoughts and beliefs take away from the quality of our lives.

In the pages of this book, you'll find practical philosophies, techniques, and methodologies that you can use to make your drumming a much more enjoyable experience. Ideally, after reading and putting the concepts into practice, you'll become a more confident, relaxed, and competent drummer. Plus, you'll find yourself playing with a greater feeling of joy in your heart.

Some of the techniques are simple, while others are a little more complex. In either case, you'll need to practice them regularly in order for the methods to work at their peak efficiency. You may have already put in countless hours of physical practice on your drumset in order to reach a certain level of proficiency, but you'll need to woodshed with your mind too. It will be worth your investment of time.

Enjoy the journey!

Bernie Schallehn

Chapter 1: The VAK Model

> *"But how do I start for the Emerald City?" asked Dorothy. "It's always best to start at the beginning," answered Glinda, the Good Witch Of The North.*
> —*from* The Wizard Of Oz *by L. Frank Baum*

When you think, how do you think? The healing art of Neuro-Linguistic Programming (NLP) gave us an answer to this question: the VAK model.

First, an explanation of terms:

V represents *video*, things you see in your mind.

A stands for *audio*, the way you hear in your mind.

K is the first letter of the word *kinesthetic*, which means the sensations on the inside and outside of your body (physical pain, hunger, touch, etc.), but, most important, it represents your emotions—your inward feelings.

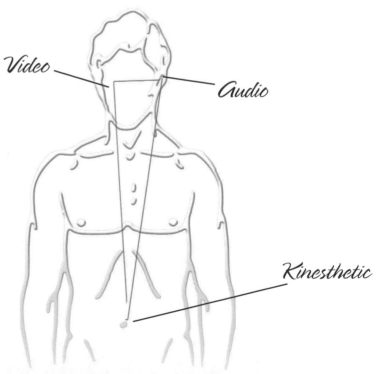

Here's how the VAK model works:

Think about a pair of drumsticks. How do they show up in your mind? Most likely as a picture, sort of like a photograph, right? Okay, now think about taking those sticks, sitting behind your drumkit, and playing your favorite beat. Can you hear in your mind the music you're creating? If you're having any difficulty with this exercise, simply close your eyes—that should make things a little easier.

Because what you're now creating in your mind is in motion—dancing on the pedals, keeping time on the hi-hats, slamming backbeats on the snare, hitting a cymbal—what you're watching is like a movie.

Finally, how does it *feel* while you're watching this movie? Joyful? Fun? Exciting? (If it's not a positive, feel-good emotion, don't worry. We'll contend with that later in the book).

Let's do another one. Think about a loved one. *Whoosh!* I bet this person immediately appeared in your mind as either a picture or a movie. Now add the dimension of sound. Hear your loved one talking to you, saying nice things. Now check how you feel in your body, your gut. Warm? Pleasant? Loved? Good!

One last illustration: Pretend the clock is heading toward noon. You feel your stomach growling—you're hungry! Your gut then sends a message to your head. Now you might see a mental image of a cheeseburger, fries, and a soda. Or a little voice inside your head might say, "I'm starving."

Your visual, audio, and kinesthetic components are always communicating with each other. A thought can begin in any one of these three places. (Please commit these essential facts of the VAK model to memory.)

Now let's jump into applying the VAK model to overcome some common barriers to good drumming. Make believe that you have your first gig with a new band. Because you haven't had the time to learn the material as well as you would have liked—due to family obligations, work, school, sickness, or whatever—you're a little shaky on about a third of the band's repertoire. There's no turning back, though. The engagement is locked in, time has run out for any additional practice, and your bandmates are depending on you to deliver the goods.

As the day of the gig approaches, a little voice in your head starts teasing you, saying, "You're not ready. You're really going to screw this up big time. You're going to blow it for the band." (Pop quiz: This thought is coming to you in _____ form. If you answered *auditory*, you're right.)

Tune in to this voice inside your head. Is it authoritative, like hearing the voice of your old high school vice principal? Is it smarmy, like when some mean-spirited classmate or coworker bullied you or poked fun at a shirt or shoes you were wearing? Or is it the voice of a scared little kid?

In most instances it's the frightened child you hear. Whatever the character, that voice sends info to the visual part of your mind and/or the body, specifically your gut, the primary residence of the physical aspect of your emotions and feelings. The result is that you start to manufacture movies of mayhem in your mind where you really mess up and blow the entire gig. You may see images of your bandmates shooting dirty looks at you, or you may hear audience members laughing hysterically as you stumble through the songs. Depending upon how strong these voices and images are, you may feel anywhere from a few butterflies in your stomach to intense nausea.

So how do you fix this situation, which is really just a horror show that you've invented in your mind? You can intervene in any of the three places—auditory, visual, or kinesthetic. Let's go with auditory first.

If you hear negative mental comments in an authoritative voice, match it with a countering message. If the authoritative voice says, "You're not ready. You're really going to screw this up big time. You're going to blow it for the band," respond inside your head with a matching tone. You might try something like this: "I may not be as ready as I'd like to be, but what evidence do I have to suggest that I'm going to screw anything up or blow it for the band?"

If you hear a bullying voice that's trying to intimidate you, here's a possible retort that you should imagine in a tough-sounding timbre: "Back off! You don't know what you're talking about. You don't scare me!"

If the doubtful messages come through in a scared child's voice, make sure your internal speech is that of a comforting adult—a parent, a big brother or sister, or a favorite uncle or aunt. Tell yourself, "It's going to be okay. You're a good drummer. And even if you haven't practiced as much for this job, you've got the skills to do a good job. You've put in a lot of practice time to get where you are today. That was time well spent, and it'll get you through this with no problems."

You can also intervene on a visual level. The following simple but effective exercise can be performed with your eyes open or closed. The idea is to construct a "success video." See yourself playing the gig—and playing it well. You can make it as if you're watching the video on TV, or as if you're looking out from your drum throne into the audience. See this mind movie in bright colors. And bring in some other senses, like the feeling of the sticks in your hands, the sound of the audience's applause, or the movement of your body as you go into a fill or hit a cymbal.

Finally, let's break these negative thoughts on a kinesthetic level. If your mental stress has caused some type of gastric issue—a stomachache, nausea, or even vomiting—try putting a heating pad on your gut. Imagine that your tight stomach has a knot in it. Untie the knot.

You can also perform some relaxation exercises. (I'll teach you those later in the book). Physical exercise of any kind will help relieve stress as well. It's helpful to follow up your exercise session with a hot shower or bath, which will further unwind an uptight body. When muscles relax, your body sends a message to the auditory and visual parts of your mind that says, "I feel calm, so everything's cool. It's going to be okay."

With all these suggestions, it's a matter of trial and outcome. If you don't get the desired results, keep at it. Experiment with different vocal tones, wording, visuals, or anything that might cause a change in your body (kinesthetic) resulting in a positive outcome. In the previous scenario, this would equate to arriving at the gig feeling a bit—or a lot—more confident about how the event is going to play out.

In an effort to deepen your understanding of the VAK model, read through the following sections, which cover a few common—if not universal—barriers to enjoyable drumming.

Competitive Feelings Toward Other Drummers

Humans are competitive by nature. Cavemen competed for women, food, and a cave that had cable TV. Look at the preponderance of competitive sports that we play or watch: baseball, basketball, billiards, boating, boxing, car racing, figure skating, football, golf, hockey, skiing, tennis, ultimate fighting…. Also consider some folks' love for competitive games, all the way from scratch-off lottery tickets, board games, and bingo to high-stakes poker, blackjack, and roulette.

Competition brings with it one primary element: the prospect of winning or losing. As musicians, we're all in this together. With the exception of competing against other drummers at an audition or a talent contest, competitive feelings toward other drummers aren't helpful. If you want to compete, compete against yourself. Set up challenges to better your skills and your groove on a daily basis.

Let's work with the following scenario. Pretend that you and your bandmates have the night off and have decided to hit the town to check out the competition on the local club scene. (Yes, I used the word *competition*.) In most cities or towns, there are limited venues to play in and seemingly unlimited numbers of bands vying for jobs. The difference here is that it's band competing against band. There's nothing one on one, unless you've fixated on the drummers in the other bands and you harbor feelings of competition toward them.

I'll explore this at length in a later chapter, but the main reason why you feel competitive toward other drummers comes from a place of your own inadequacy.

But what does it mean to be "better" than another drummer? Do you have better four-limb independence? Are your hands faster? Or is it that you own a kit that's bigger, newer, or of better quality than the next guy's?

Do you judge the technical wizard Thomas Lang to be a better drummer than the Rolling Stones' Charlie Watts? Should Ringo hang up his sticks because Carter Beauford is ambidextrous?

I hope you don't feel this way. There's a place for everyone in the universe of drumming, and everyone is entitled to play in his or her own style.

All right, let's get back to your night on the town. If, when you watch another band rip into its first few tunes, you have a problem with feeling competitive toward the other drummer, a little voice (audio) will usually say one of two things:

"This drummer sucks. I'm better than him."

"This drummer is really good. I suck."

In this competition, neither one of you wins. If you judge the other drummer to be subpar, you're sending out negative vibes to a fellow artist who's probably playing to the best of his or her ability. Why wouldn't you want to support someone who shares your love and passion for drumming? Again, we're all in this together. And, just like you, this other drummer has practiced for many hours to acquire a certain skill set.

If you judge yourself to be a lousy drummer in comparison with the person on stage, you lose. Your harsh remarks cut a deep slice into your self-confidence.

Here's how to intervene in this situation, using the VAK model. We'll start with your mentally bashing the other guy on the riser.

On a video level, make a mind movie of this drummer practicing at home. Watch him struggle—just as you have—with certain rhythms and fills.

On an audio level, speak some words internally, such as: "Hey, all props to this guy up there. He's doing his best. Maybe on their break, I'll tell him I enjoyed his drumming."

If you've worked on these visual or audio levels, you should automatically start to feel a connection (kinesthetic) with your fellow drummer.

Now let's reverse the situation. You walk into the club and are totally intimidated by the other drummer's advanced skills. Your internal voice now bashes *you*. Let's offset that using VAK.

Visually, recall a time when you were playing at your finest. See the audience applauding your efforts.

On your internal audio channel, dial in the following: "This guy is excellent! Man, I bet he's put in years of practice to get to this level. He and his drums speak in a different voice that's not better than mine, just different. There'll always be a place for my own unique drumming."

If you've been successful with your visual and auditory work, your kinesthetic sense should automatically be feeling some pleasant sensations. Drift away from your internal audio and visualizations, and return to the moment. Become just another member of the audience, enjoying and grooving to the music. The other drummer may be superb, but experience him as a part of the whole and not as a separate entity.

Philosophically, I ask that you consider thinking of your drumming from a contribution standpoint, rather than a competitive one. What can your unique voice contribute to the universe of music and drumming?

Good Days Versus Bad Days

I'll begin by defining specifically what I mean by good days versus bad days, as they relate to your drumming. Whether you're engaged in practicing by yourself in your rehearsal space, working up a new tune at band rehearsal, or performing for 20,000 adoring fans, what are the visuals, audio, and kinesthetics connected with both good and bad days?

When you're having a good day, all is right in the world. Your hands, arms, and feet are relaxed and feel as if there isn't a beat you couldn't play or a fill you couldn't nail. You're timing is spot-on; you *are* the click. Perhaps there's a feeling of physical power coursing through your body. You're glowing, flowing, and your drumming feels effortless. (This is your kinesthetic sense—what you feel, on the inside and outside of your body.)

Aurally, you're hearing sounds and voices inside and outside your head. The music you're making is heavenly, and your stick draws the perfect tones from the drumheads. Your cymbals shimmer with sound, either when you're keeping time on the hi-hat or when your stick flashes effortlessly through the air to strike a crash or splash.

There may be a voice inside your head running commentary on how well you're playing. The voice is, most likely, upbeat and strong—complimenting you in bold terms. Or, should you have a more laid-back personality, your internal voice is talking to you in a calm and confident manner, telling you what a great job you're doing, while encouraging you to keep going.

If you're gigging, you may be looking out into a sea of smiling faces, whether it's three or three thousand people. Your audience is responding to you and reacting to the music you're making. It's an equal give-and-take experience. You're putting energy out there, and they're handing it back to you. Heads and bodies are moving in time to the music you're creating. You catch a glance, a smile or grin from one of your bandmates, and the unspoken message is, "Bro, you're in the pocket!"

Inner visuals may or may not be there. In this situation, the kinesthetic and auditory senses tend to prevail. If you're seeing anything at all, perhaps you're previewing future good days, believing that every practice session or gig could be this fantastic. My suggestion is to savor where you are right now. Live in the moment and truly enjoy this good day. When good days happen, or when you create them, savor every millisecond of the experience.

On the opposite side of the spectrum, there are a million reasons why you might be having a bad day. For illustrative purposes, I'll present a few. Let's imagine that on a kinesthetic level you just don't feel well. Perhaps it's fatigue, the flu, or food poisoning, or your body is sore and achy from overdoing it in a game of touch football with your buds.

On the inside, let's imagine that you're recovering from a loss of some kind. You're feeling quite sad. (A bad day could also be caused by a host of other emotions, including anxiety, boredom, and frustration.) Maybe you've recently ended a relationship with someone you love, and it hurts deep inside. Or, sadder yet, death has taken a parent, a favorite uncle or aunt, or one of your best friends.

Sometimes you simply can't pin down why you're having a bad day. You just *are*. You suffer through a practice session or group rehearsal while feeling low. Your coordination, timing, and feel are way off, and nothing you play sounds good. Mercifully, the practice session ends, and maybe you retreat to your room and flop on the bed.

The problem, however, is that you have a gig tonight. So unless you cancel or find a replacement, you've got to deliver the goods come show-time.

The best way to help yourself heal during one of these down days is to do something nice and soothing for your body. Take a long, hot bath. Spend some cash on a massage. Sit in a sauna. Call in sick to your day job if you need to, and spend the day in your pajamas watching TV or listening to some mellow jazz. Doze off. Do anything you think might help your body experience more good feelings than bad.

While you're relaxing, construct some mind movies where you see yourself playing adequately that night. Better yet, perform your visualizations as if you're actually there as an active participant in the gig. The comfortable, pleasant feelings you're experiencing physically while you're taking a bath or relaxing on the couch will become associated with the mind movies of sitting behind your kit and playing the gig that night.

Notice that I suggested performing a visualization of playing the gig adequately. You're certainly free to visualize a stellar performance. But since you're not feeling all that well, and the soothing effects of the bath might wear off by gig time, it's a good idea to safeguard the situation with a visualization in which you assure yourself that you're going to make it through. It's your choice.

What you say to yourself—your internal self-talk—is very important in dealing with good days and bad days. If you keep reinforcing how bad you feel by thinking, "Man, I ache all over. How am I going to make it through the gig?" you'll make yourself feel even lousier, and there's a strong possibility that you'll create an internal environment that will result in a subpar night of drumming. (If you haven't noticed by now, I'm using a lot of words and phrases that lend themselves to the idea that you are—in many ways, but not all ways—responsible for the way you feel and act.)

Here are a few things you could say to yourself to counter negative self-talk:

"Yep, I do ache, but that doesn't mean I can't play the songs."

"I know these tunes! I'll just get out of my own head and allow my muscle memory to take over."

"Life is time limited; this gig is time limited. With each song performed, I get closer to the end of the night."

"So what if I don't play my finest tonight? I care about my band and the music, but physical maladies happen to everyone. If my bandmates ask, I'll share with them the fact that I'm feeling a bit ill, but only if they ask. I might play just fine. We'll have to wait and see."

Handling an emotional bad day, like when you're dealing with loss and sadness, is a bit tougher to overcome. Use the same kinesthetic approaches—hot bath, sauna, etc.—and the same visuals, but know that the self-talk may have to be a bit more profound.

Here are some things you could say to yourself to help overcome these feelings of loss and sadness:

"My dad is proud of me and what I've accomplished. He's looking down on me from heaven and smiling."

"I miss Ashley, but when the time feels right, I'll start dating again. I will find someone else."

"Uncle Bob was my favorite, but I have my memories, and he'll always live on in my heart."

Contending with an internal bad day often involves dealing with distracting or intrusive thoughts in visual and/or auditory formats. Here's a quick but effective exercise you can use.

On a small slip of paper, write a statement that is the essence of the person, place, or thing that's causing your emotional bad day. For example: "My parents are divorcing, and I'm really sad." Writing it down helps to externalize it. Now fold the paper as many times as you can and put it somewhere—in a small box, a desk drawer, or between the pages of a book. Now walk away from it. Know that it's there, but it's away from you. You can reconnect with it after the gig…if you so desire.

Here are two final thoughts regarding good days versus bad days:

1. Immerse yourself in your drumming. Be there—physically, mentally, emotionally, and spiritually. There's a story of a world-class drummer who was on tour in the States. Minutes before he was to play for thousands at an outdoor venue, he learned of his father's death back in England. When his cue came, he took his seat behind his kit. Later, he told a reporter that he had mentally dedicated his performance to his dad and then immersed himself in the task at hand.

2. If you're having a bad day, cut yourself some slack! You're only human. What's the worst that could happen? No one is going to take

your birthday away or send you to a hard labor camp if you don't play well.

It's important to study and get comfortable with the VAK model, as it's the foundation that everything else in this book will be built on. Commit to memory the illustration of the head and torso. Video and audio are in your head; kinesthetics—feelings on the inside and outside—are in your body.

Chapter 2: Motivation

"A strong passion for any object will ensure success,
for the desire of the end will point out the means."

—Ben Stein

Now that you have a firm grasp of the VAK model, let's continue our journey with a question: Why did you choose to become a drummer?

Notice I didn't say "play the drums," because there's a certain distancing quality in phrasing it in that way. Obviously, if you have a full- or part-time job as, say, a dishwasher you're more likely to say, "I wash dishes," rather than, "I'm a dishwasher." That style of terminology doesn't define you. It merely states what you do rather than who you are.

I'm hoping you're proud to be a drummer and that you use that term when describing an aspect of your being.

Now let's proceed with a few more questions. (I'm going to assume you've been a drummer for at least a month or two.)

How did you make the choice to be a drummer? Did you watch a band—live or on TV—and find yourself fixated on the drums? Were lessons offered in school and you were lucky enough to snag one of the spots as a snare drummer in the concert band? Or were you born into a family of drummers and percussionists and it was simply a given that you would grow up to become one yourself?

In the 1960s, I was in my early teens, and everyone played a rock 'n' roll instrument—drums, bass, guitar, or keyboards. I remember hardware stores selling cheap drumsets and no-name guitars because the demand was so great. You could even order guitars, amps, and drums out of Montgomery Ward and Sears catalogs. This was during the time of the British Invasion, with bands like the Beatles, the Rolling Stones, the Dave Clark Five, Herman's Hermits, and Gerry & the Pacemakers being played all over the airwaves and featured in the pages of popular media. Once you could play an instrument—even with just a little skill—you joined or formed a band.

The first drums I played were my friend's red Kents. I was immediately hooked and begged my parents for formal lessons. My folks agreed and allowed me to sign on for three one-hour lessons a week. My first drum teacher was a guy we'll call Billy. Billy was a good drummer and a good instructor, but you never wanted to have the last lesson of the night. (Billy traded flams and rolls with hits off a mug of beer that always stayed full, so by the later hours his speech, playing, and instruction were all a little "liquid.")

The first song I mastered was Herman's Hermits' "I'm Henry The VIII, I Am." I played that song until my muscles cramped, and the neighbors complained more than once about my late-into-the-night rehearsals.

Billy might have had a slight drinking problem, but I thought what he did with all his students after six months of private lessons was brilliant: He cut you loose. With a stern look, he'd say, "I've taught you the basics—now go find your own voice." He might have been a lousy businessman, but he was a master of motivation. By dismissing us as students, we were faced with choices:

1. Quit.

2. Continue our education informally by playing along to records and the radio or by seeking out drum books to study from.

3. Find another private instructor.

4. Join the concert or marching band in school or audition for a drum corps outside of school.

Billy taught us the basics, and by setting us free he forced us to answer these questions: Do I want to stick with drumming? Does drumming have enough of a hold on me for me to seek out other ways to learn? Am I willing to make the investment of time and energy to keep going?

This brings us to a point of discussion on motivation. Motivation is either pleasure based or pain based, or it's a combination of the two. You brush your teeth because you like that clean feeling (kinesthetic) and you like how white they look when you brush them regularly (external and internal video). That's pleasure-based motivation. It feels good, it looks good, and you like the outcome. And because you like it, the behavior tends to be self-reinforcing. You perform the task, faithfully, every morning and night.

You also brush your teeth because you want to avoid cavities, rotting gums, and bad breath. This is an example of pain-based motivation. You don't want these things to occur, so you scrub away. Brushing your teeth is actually a combination of both pleasure- and pain-based motivation.

Now think about income taxes. If you're due for a refund, you probably file in January because you want that check. If you owe the government money, however, or you simply know it's the law to file before April 15, you (like most of us) have to force yourself to get those taxes done—begrudgingly and with a bit of stalling. That's pain-based motivation. Why? Because you know that if you fail to file, there's a chance you'll go to jail or have to pay a hefty fine.

Here's a quick way to remember the two types of motivation:

Pleasure-based—moving *toward* the behavior, object, or situation.
Pain-based—moving *away* from the behavior, object, or situation.

Motivation is a critical element in being a drummer. I've read biographies of famous musicians whose parents forced them to bang away endlessly on a piano or blow into an oboe until they were blue in the face. But somewhere along the journey something took hold of them and they began to love their instrument. They started to adore the sounds they were creating and began to enjoy the process of making music. Unless you're strongly motivated to become—and remain—a drummer, you'll likely find your kit collecting dust and then going up for sale on eBay or Craigslist.

Let's take a look at some of the specific reasons why motivation can falter and sometimes fail you as a drummer.

Not Progressing Fast Enough
We live in a fast-paced world. Think of the term *multitasking*, a process whereby you're expected to perform many jobs or responsibilities in one block of time. Using your VAK model, visualize a middle-age business-

man chattering away in rapid, clipped speech on a cell phone while one hand frantically clicks something on his computer screen and the other hand juggles a dripping slice of pizza.

When I think about that scenario, a little voice inside my head says, "Too much!" while my stomach twists into a knot of tension (kinesthetic).

In order to become proficient as a drummer, you need to slow down and focus your full attention on the task at hand in each practice session or performance. For some fledgling drummers, if they're not playing super-fast blast beats after two weeks of lessons, they get angry, frustrated, and are ready to quit. Others feel that if they don't nail a song in practice after one or two attempts, they're a failure.

Harboring those sorts of expectations constitutes what's known as erroneous or irrational thinking. When you're not progressing at the warp-speed rate you've set for yourself, the voice inside your head often sums it up accordingly: "I stink as a drummer."

Let's tear apart this irrational, erroneous thinking. In Malcolm Gladwell's best-selling book *Outliers: The Story Of Success*, neurologist Daniel Levitin writes: "The emerging picture from studies is that ten thousand hours of practice is required to achieve the level of mastery associated with being a world-class expert—in anything."

You attend a drum clinic at your local music store and a world-class drummer is burning up the stage. One part of you is blown away by this drummer's chops; another part of you hears a little voice inside your head that says, "I'll never be that good."

Don't bail on your kit if, after just a few months' time, you're not flailing away expertly like your favorite drummer. Take it one day at a time, and see what happens.

Here's a metaphor you might find helpful when applied to progress on your drumkit: You're on one side of a lake and want to row to the other. You have a small boat and a set of oars. With each pull on the oars you make progress in achieving your goal of reaching the other side of the lake. It's not necessarily easy; perhaps you find it to be hard work, and from time to time you need to rest. But with each pull on the oars, you're steadily gliding through the water and making progress.

Now, some critical questions that you must answer in total honesty:

Am I willing to put in the time and energy and make the necessary sacrifices that are associated with progressing as a drummer?

Am I willing to contend with society's perception of a musician in my quest to become the best drummer I can be?

Do my family, friends, and/or significant other support my quest to progress in my art?

What do I want to get out of drumming, and how far do I want to go in the professional world of music?

Have I written down my specific drumming goals?

Time, Energy, And Sacrifices

John Lennon once wrote, "Life is what happens to you while you're busy making other plans." You may have written down the goal of being a professional musician, and you have the best intentions of practicing six hours a day. The problem for most of us is that we have school or a day job to contend with. So how do you deal with this situation?

The key is to maximize the time you have with your drums. Whether you can allot ten minutes or ten hours a day, be at your kit as often as you can. Let your family and friends know that this time is important, and that you need to be free of distraction.

There's been much written about how to spend your practice time, so I'm not going to address that issue here. Whether you're studying rudiments, jamming along to recorded music, or simply freestyling, play with joy and love in your heart. It's important to have an attitude of gratitude anytime you sit behind your kit. You're lucky to have the physical health, ability, time, and resources to engage in a session with these beautiful instruments. Contemplate that concept for a while.

There are elements of self-discipline and energy investment that come with acquiring and maintaining any skill. Drums are no different. Undoubtedly, there will be some days—maybe even weeks—when you just don't feel like practicing. This is the time when you need to just suck it up and do it. You'll likely phase into a flowing state that will make your time at the kit no longer feel like a chore.

Certain motivational experts espouse the philosophy that some people "need to feel the heat rather than see the light." This approach can work when someone is avoiding treatment for a severe drug addiction and is on the brink of losing everything, but I'd rather not use it here. Frightening yourself into a practice session by imagining a nightmarish internal video of a disastrous stage performance can cause you to associate a negative relationship with your drums, which will make you feel uptight and nervous.

With addicts, sure, let them know what they stand to lose if they don't seek treatment. I, however, prefer to apply the idea that the motivational training pioneer Napoleon Hill told audiences in pursuit of a goal: "Keep your mind on the things you want and off the things you don't want." If you want to get through a practice session in order to keep your chops up and continue to progress, then don't continue to focus on how averse you are to picking up the sticks to start the process.

You have the ability in many situations to steer your thoughts the way you want them to go. You're not a passive recipient of random thoughts that lead to behaviors. Grab hold of the wheel and drive!

Following Hill's advice, make a short mind movie of a future gig where you're soloing at a big venue. You can hear the shouts and screams of approval from the audience (auditory), which inspire you to play faster, stronger, and with even more charisma. Every cell, fiber, and muscle in your body is on fire. You've never played better, and you're bursting with confidence, skill, and power. The solo ends, and as you catch your breath you know that you got to this point because of the time you spent practicing your instrument. Doesn't that feel awesome! (This is an example of pleasure-based motivation.)

Keep in mind that most things in life involve a trade-off. If you're married with children, time on your kit is time away from your kids. If you're a student, perhaps you should be studying or just hanging with friends to blow off steam. If your motivation to become a better drummer is true and stays strong, though, you'll be willing to make these trade-offs.

Work, Love, Play
Invest time in all three of these, but strive to find a balance. When I refer

to work, I'm speaking of your day job or your status as a student or full-time musician. Love is found in many relationships—whether it's romantic, fatherly, motherly, brotherly, or sisterly. Play could mean drumming or tossing around a football with your friends.

Sometimes these spheres of work, love, and play get out of balance and become lopsided. If you're struggling with your physics class, studying has kept you away from your instrument. If your boss has assigned you a big project at work and you've been staying late at the office in an attempt to finish it on schedule, there's likely no time left for drumming. If your connection with your significant other is starting to nose-dive and you need to invest time in repairing any damage or deciding to end the relationship, finding the chance to play even a couple flams could be nearly impossible.

All of us are given twenty-four hours each day—no more, no less. The key word here is *strive*. Strive to find a balance of work, love, and play.

To end this section, let's deal with a concept that you may find a little frightening. I'm talking about sacrifice. If your motivation to become a professional drummer is strong enough, you might have to sacrifice time in other aspects of your life. This decision could lead to life-changing consequences. I've seen drummers sacrifice romantic relationships, high-paying jobs with great benefits, and the basic security of having enough money to pay bills—all for the love of art. No one can make that decision but you. If you know that expressing yourself through drumming is what you're supposed to be doing on this earth, then go for it. I wish you the very best of luck.

Societal Views Of The Drummer

A manager walks into a nightclub with the intention of booking his band. The club owner asks him, "How many musicians in your group?" The manager replies, "Four, plus a drummer."

Have you ever seen those little metal wind-up toys with a character clanging cymbals together or alternating strokes on a snare drum with tiny sticks? Did you pay close attention to what the character was? It was most likely a monkey. Or maybe it was a clown.

When Jim Henson invented the Muppets, what name did he give to the drummer? Animal.

How often are drummers drawn as intelligent, creative, and stable individuals on par with all the other musicians in the band? Very rarely. What I've tended to see are knuckle-dragging, mouth-breathing cretins who bash away on a kit like a Neanderthal.

In real life, drummers who are lucky enough to be featured on the cover of a major music magazine are often photographed with their tongue sticking out or posing with their best "badass" look. I can understand that certain types of music might warrant this image, but consider your average Joe passing by the newsstand and seeing that type of face glaring back at him. The photo perpetuates the stereotype.

To the best of my knowledge, no one has invented the guitar equivalent of a drum practice pad. Why were practice pads invented? It's because drums, by nature, are very loud instruments. And often the word *loud* has negative connotations, like "loud and obnoxious."

My point is that these depictions of drummers and drumming have seeped into the collective unconscious and, unfortunately, have marred our profession to make us appear less skilled than other musicians. This, in turn, can diminish our motivation to play an instrument that's associated with being basic, simplistic, and not very respectable.

I recently ran across an old Leedy Drum Company advertisement with a pen-and-ink drawing of a smiling drummer promoting a new drumset. The caption read: "Easy to play!" Nothing could be further from the truth. Granted, in a short time span most people can learn to play a very basic beat. But as you delve deeper into the art, think of all the skills you need to become proficient at drumming: timing and meter, four-limb independence, dynamic control, groove and fill vocabulary, proper hand and foot technique…. This list can go on forever. Plus you'll need to learn how to weave your drumming into the fabric of a band so that the ensemble will sound like a cohesive unit.

In a global sense, there exists a conflict between acceptable societal norms and the artist's life. Society wants conformity. Society wants you to have a briefcase, a pension plan, and two weeks of paid vacation—it wants you to conform to the norm. But maybe your idea of the good life is touring the country in an old Ford Econoline van with your friends and playing every nightclub that will book you. So what if your wardrobe consists of T-shirts, jeans, and Chuck Taylor sneakers? You're happy!

The reality is that the majority of performing musicians are weekend warriors. If that's your situation, relish those Friday- and Saturday-night gigs. But if you want to try your hand at being a full-time musician, I say go for it! To quote philosopher Joseph Campbell, "Follow your bliss." As far as I know, no one has ever lamented on his or her deathbed about not spending enough time at the office. If, however, you have a nice blend of a fulfilling day job and a weekend band that satisfies your artistic needs, you're very fortunate. Keep that attitude-of-gratitude mentality front and center.

Support From Family And Friends

We're all born into a family unit, and we all live and die in one. Initially, it's our mom, dad, and any number of siblings. As we grow up and move out of that family of origin, we make a new one. Most of us find a mate and then start the next generation.

How our family—especially our parents—reacts to our love of drumming plays a huge part in our motivation. Although my parents paid for my lessons and bought me a Ludwig Club Date kit, they were very frightened of what might come next. During high school, they generously opened their house for Sunday-afternoon rehearsals for my high school rock bands, but they were suspicious of the musicians who came to the practices.

For most parents, the three major fears they harbor for their adolescents are unplanned pregnancy, drug and alcohol abuse, and car crashes. When my band started playing at high school dances and youth centers, my folks' fear of drug abuse began to escalate. A lot of their apprehensions were based on drummers from their generation who had been busted for substance use. I made sure I never came home after a gig under the influence of alcohol, and I never committed any infractions that my parents could have connected with drumming.

Despite my efforts, my mom and dad's fears skyrocketed when I attended college. I was now old enough to be playing in clubs where—according to them—seedy characters tended to congregate. But the mother of all fears for them was that I would love playing music so much that I would abandon college altogether. Their solution was to make sure that each summer I came home and got a "real" summer job. If I refused, they'd pull my tuition money. I wanted to stay in college and also keep drumming, so at the end of each spring semester I'd quit the band I was in and dutifully come home to work a job.

I realize now that my parents' strategy was borne out of love and concern, but it made things difficult because with each successive year of college, I had to find a new band. The one positive to this experience was that it strengthened my resolve to keep drumming. It was tough going, but drumming was so important to me that I could tolerate the resistance I was subjected to at home.

When I was thirty-five, the wedding band I was playing with was hired to play at my cousin's reception. My parents came to the wedding, and they saw me play. That was the first time they had seen me perform in public. My dad heaped on the compliments. I was never happier and never more proud. (I guess by that point, with a wife and two kids at home, I had, my folks figured, escaped all the evils that drumming could have brought into my life.)

If you're a teenager or young adult, don't come home from a gig drunk or stoned. If you're engaged or married, the same advice applies, along with not succumbing to other temptations. Your misbehaviors will inevitably be associated with your drumming, and you'll have to work hard to reestablish a broken bond of trust. Plus, support from loved ones is very helpful, especially if you enter a period where motivation for your art falters.

Your friends play a part in your motivation to start and continue your involvement with music. If you're already playing in a band, you'll automatically receive support because you're surrounded by people of similar interests. It's with your friends outside your musical circle where you may encounter resistance. If you've just graduated high school or college, it's likely that many of your friends will soon enter into the world of nine-to-five work.

Consciously and unconsciously, your family and friends have been socialized and influenced to believe that health plans, commissions, and the security of a day job are your destiny, too. That may come true someday, but what if right now you want to tour around the country with your band? I say follow your heart and follow your dreams. The reactions from friends may vary. You might be on the receiving end of some anger, most likely because some of your friends lack the courage to pursue their passions, and jealousy has reared its ugly head. Others may dismiss you as immature or as a slacker who's afraid to enter into the real world with all of its adult responsibilities. But your true friends—the ones who really love and care about you—will support your decision no matter what.

We'll close this section with a quote from the twentieth-century painter Georgia O'Keeffe: "I've been absolutely terrified every moment of my life—and I've never let it keep me from doing a single thing I wanted to do."

Hitting Plateaus

Feeling stuck at a certain level in your drumming can seriously impact your motivation to keep playing. Plateaus can make you feel that you lack the ability to progress, or that the thrill is gone, or a combination of the two. Plateaus come in two varieties—short term and long term.

Short-Term Plateaus

You're at your kit practicing, and it's just not happening. Maybe your bandleader sent you an MP3 of a new song and you just can't nail the intro. You yank the headphones off your ears and hear a little voice inside your head, threatening you: "I'm gonna quit. I just can't do it."

You've reached a short-term plateau. In most instances, with thought, patience, and practice, you'll eventually master that intro. But the experience of not being able to learn a part to this new song as quickly as you feel you should baffles you and gives rise to strong negative emotions and self-doubt. It's a dangerous state to be in, because it can snowball if the little voice in your head that first convinced you of being incapable of executing the intro then generalizes to other musical challenges that lie ahead.

When you were an infant, first you learned how to crawl. Then you progressed to walking. There was never any doubt in your infant mind that you wouldn't succeed at this venture. You just kept moving forward until you acquired the skill. And when you were learning to speak, first you babbled, and then you learned how to say words. Here again, there were never any thoughts of failure regarding the skill.

Granted, when you were learning to walk, you fell—a lot. But walking is what you inherently wanted to do, so you kept at it doggedly until you succeeded. If you ask your parents, most likely they'll remember that you often got angry and frustrated when you were first beginning to talk. You were unintelligible for a period of time, but eventually you started making sense, and those around you were no longer asking, "What did you say, honey?"

So what happened to that unfaltering, unwavering belief in yourself? Here's a little clue: "No!"

As you were growing up, you heard the word *no* tens of thousands of times. You heard it from your parents, your teachers, other adults, and even your friends. Some of the time the word was used out of necessity and may even have helped you to survive so you could grow up to become a drummer.

"No! Don't touch the burners on the stove!"

"No! Don't eat that berry—it's poisonous!"

"No! You can't jump out your bedroom window. You're not Spider-Man!"

But as many times as you heard the good *no*, you also heard at least one use of the word that damaged your belief in yourself.

"No, you're not going to try out for the football team—you're not big enough and you'll get hurt."

"No, you're not going to audition for the school musical. I've heard you sing, and you'd embarrass yourself."

"No, I'm not really interested in having a relationship. I'm just not that into you."

Think back to a time when *no* held you back. It stings, doesn't it? And many times you didn't even have the opportunity to try the behavior to see if you'd succeed or fail. Unfortunately, many of those little *no* seeds grew into self-limiting beliefs that continue to haunt you to this day. Self-limiting beliefs are rooted in lack, scarcity, and powerlessness.

Let's steer it the other way. Hear the next sentence in your own voice inside your head: "Yes, I can." In that three-word sentence, you initiate more self-empowerment than you'll ever know.

Helen Keller, a woman who was born blind and deaf but overcame incredible obstacles and went on to lead a full and inspirational life, once said, "We can do anything we want to do if we stick to it long enough." So let's return to the situation where you were struggling with that intro. Put yourself back in the practice session where you're telling yourself you can't do it and you're threatening to quit drumming. Before you put your headphones back on, close your eyes and do a quick recall of all the successes you've had in your life. For most of us, the successes far out-number the failures.

Whenever you attempt to learn something new—in this case the intro to the song—frustration and its best friend, anger, aren't far away. They're just itching to get you to react in a nonproductive way. Skill acquisition happens at different rates for each of us. Sometimes it's tied closely to the amount of time and quality of practice, but not always. In any event, take a deep breath and relax. When you relax, anger and frus-tration subside and you're left with the opportunity to give that intro another go.

Try *easy*. We've all heard the phrase *try hard* countless times, but *try easy* works much better. Here's why: When you try hard, your body has a propensity to become uptight (your muscles tighten in response to those words), and your mind becomes anxious. Trying hard usually results in slowing down the acquisition of the skill. You're uptight, and anxiety blocks concentration. Instead, believe that you can do it, relax, and stay loose.

Here's an illustration of this better way of thinking and doing:

Take a pen and hold it tightly in your fingers. Really squeeze it—hard! Now write your name on a piece of paper. Your fingers may hurt and your signature may look childlike or unrecognizable. Now try easy. Take the pen in your hand like you have thousands of times before. Hold it securely but don't strangle it, and write your name. The pain in your fingers is gone, and your signature is written in your normal handwriting.

Now put on your headphones and try easy at learning that song's intro.

Long-Term Plateaus

Feeling stuck at a drumming plateau on a long-term basis—a time period of weeks or months—can come from a number of sources. Let's explore a few.

Boredom

If you're playing in a band where the repertoire never changes, boredom could be fooling you into believing you've hit a plateau. I say "fooling" because with a band whose act never changes, the members never have the opportunity to challenge themselves or grow as musicians. At some point, you make an assessment of your drumming, and you—erroneously—decide that it's mediocre. This has occurred because you've been grinding out the same tunes night after night, never having the opportunity to change things up. With no challenges, there's a good chance you're going to get bored. Perhaps you don't even practice anymore. Why bother? You know what's expected of you once you hit the stage.

So what's the solution? See if you can get the bandleader to add a few new songs to your set list. If you're leading the band, bring in some new tunes, schedule a rehearsal, and let your bandmates know that they've got a bit of work to do. If you're met with resistance, you have three choices. You can stay in the band and continue to pump out the same material at every gig; you can stay in the band but challenge yourself on your own by listening to and/or practicing other styles of music; or you can leave your current band and find a more stimulating and challenging musical situation.

Distraction

Is there something, or someone, that's renting a lot of space in your head? Be honest. It happens to all of us.

Distraction can cut deeply into your motivation, as it mentally, and sometimes physically, pulls you away from your drums. When you're playing well, your total being is immersed in the process. This can be a Zen-like state where there's a lack of conscious thought, and you simply experience the sheer enjoyment of making music.

As an exercise, sit at your kit and begin playing. After five or ten minutes, stop and ask yourself, "What am I thinking about?" Are you in total immersion with your drums, or are you just going through the motions? Using your VAK model, are you aware of any pictures or movies that might be playing in your mind while you're laying down a groove? Is there a voice inside your head commenting on something other than your drumming? Even if you're not aware of any picture or voices, are you enjoying a number of positive sensations in your body, or do you feel slightly off-kilter and maybe even a bit unwell? (In this case, the internal pictures and voices might be slightly out of range for you to see or tune in to, but they have communicated kinesthetically with your gut.)

There's a host of distractions that could be snaring your attention, like work, school, boss, teacher, boyfriend, husband, girlfriend, wife, affairs, home repairs, children, friends, finances, health, drugs, alcohol, gambling, and so on. The solution to combating distractions that eat away at your motivation is simple, but not easy.

One option is to accept the situation as it is, do nothing, play on (in life as well as on your drums), and see what happens. The distraction may become tired of pestering you and just fade away.

The other option is to change the situation on the inside or on the outside. Much of this book offers ways to change things on the inside, primarily through the way you view yourself and the world. Be forewarned that change on the outside may involve some very scary actions— divorce, declaring bankruptcy, going in for medical tests, and so on. But delaying or avoiding these often unpleasant experiences is sometimes more painful than the experiences themselves.

Pretend you've got a bad toothache. You don't like going to the dentist because it's often a painful experience. Your toothache (pain-based motivation) inspires you to pick up the phone and dial the office. The receptionist offers you an appointment the following day or one in three weeks. Which appointment do you choose? If you delay, you're going to have to endure three more weeks of distracting pain. Take the appointment for the next day, and soon the whole distracting experience is over.

Should you choose to make a change, my suggestion is to deal with the situation as soon as possible. Don't delay, so you can get on with your drumming—and your life—unencumbered.

Limitations

In his song "Beautiful Despair," Rodney Crowell sings, "Beautiful despair is hearing Dylan when you're drunk at 3 A.M., knowing that the chances are, no matter what, you'll never write like him." Crowell is correct, but why would he *want* to write like Dylan? Crowell has contributed so much to the world of songwriting—all with his own words.

When I was in college, I went to see Billy Cobham with the Mahavishnu Orchestra. Cobham was behind this massive kit—double kicks, toms galore, and dozens of cymbals. I had a front-row seat and was able to watch Billy up close and personal. I'd heard him on recordings but had never seen him in concert. It was incredible. He played polyrhythms with incredible ease, and his hands and feet moved with speed, fluidity, finesse, and grace. Yet I left the concert feeling very depressed. I knew, to paraphrase Rodney Crowell's lyrics, that chances are—no matter what—I'd never play like Cobham.

My thinking has changed since then. I've contributed my drumming voice to many bands and solo artists, and I feel proud of my accomplishments. I don't have to play like Billy Cobham. I never did, and I couldn't even if I wanted to.

This may seem to contradict what I said earlier regarding the positive "Yes, I can" approach to drumming. But the truth is that there was an error in my thinking regarding the Cobham experience.

To cure this contradiction, I'm going to amend Helen Keller's statement: "We can do anything we want to do—*in our own voice*—if we stick to it long enough." I think that's closer to the truth.

I want you to always play your best and to keep evolving as a drummer, but we're all different in our playing. The praise that you might receive from an audience member who tells you, "Man, you play just like Carter Beauford," will eventually wear thin. Why? Because deep in your heart you want to be known, recognized, accepted, and complimented for your own style.

The reality is that we all have limitations—physical, mental, and emotional. Your job is to become the best you can be within your own capabilities. You can overcome many of your limitations, but there will be some that persist for a lifetime. For those, you'll need to learn to work with or around them.

I once had the pleasure of watching a young man with cerebral palsy perform an incredible drum solo. It was obvious that he had physical limitations on a neuromuscular level, because he had duct-taped sticks into his hands. The point here is that he was playing *in spite of* his limitations. And perhaps he had overcome a mental limitation after he or someone else had said, "You've got CP—you can't be a drummer." Did he play like Billy Cobham? Of course not. But he did play a solid beat that landed right in the pocket, and he was rewarded with a thunderous standing ovation at the conclusion of his solo.

Admitting to a limitation is a sign of strength, not weakness. It shows that you know who you are and you understand which abilities you possess.

In an interview in the March 2007 issue of *Modern Drummer*, Elton John percussionist John Mahon talks about recording alongside drummer Nigel Olsson. "When we played the last song, 'Captain And The Kid,'" Mahon says, "we couldn't quite figure out what to do. The producer and I talked about maybe doing a train beat with brushes. Nigel said, 'I can't do that,' so he had me do that."

That experience shows that Olsson had the confidence to admit to a limitation: He couldn't play a train beat. Notice that he didn't make excuses or attempt to fog the idea with alternative ways of playing the track. He simply handed off the duties to Mahon. No big deal.

Your Drummer Self-Esteem

Should someone pay you a compliment about your drumming, do you believe him or her? Do you own the praise? If not, then you likely suffer from low self-esteem when it comes to your drumming. In this chapter, everything relates to motivation. If you don't believe in your drumming and aren't convinced that you're at least a competent drummer, your motivation to stay with the instrument may falter or fail altogether. In the next chapter, we're going to tackle drummer self-esteem head on.

Chapter 3: Drummer Self-Esteem

"All of the significant battles are waged within the self."

—Sheldon Kopp

Are you a good drummer? Do you believe in yourself and your abilities? I'm not interested in whether you can deliver the goods in a performance or how many great venues you've played or which big-name musicians have given you a call for session work. I want you to explore and examine your deepest, most honest thoughts and feelings about your abilities.

We all have a bad night when we can't seem to hit anything right. Your timing is off, your fills are sloppy and rushed, and you can't get your bass drum foot to stroke out an even double. But overall, do you believe you're competent at your craft? If not, you've got some work to do, because low self-esteem can leak into every aspect of your playing. It can destroy your love for your art, and it can lead you down a destructive path where you end up numbing negative feelings with drugs and alcohol. Or you may end up tossing your kit out on the front lawn at your next garage sale.

When you begin to think more highly of yourself as a drummer, with your thoughts being those of confidence, competence, and increased self-esteem, the results will be astounding. Arrogance, conceit, and narcissism have no place here. We're talking about being solid in your convictions that you're a good player, no matter where you are in your musical journey—rank beginner or seasoned pro.

In his interview in the April 2008 issue of *Modern Drummer*, country star Brad Paisley's drummer, Ben Sesar, says, "For my entire life, my core has involved being aggressive and even a bit cocky." He goes on to say, "I'm not a normal studio player. I'm on the edge when I'm in there. I don't come in there with a bag of tricks, but when I'm in the moment there has to be a cockiness about the playing. I can't worry if the producer doesn't like it."

Sesar is clearly a man who believes in his drumming, and he believes he has something to offer. Notice that he doesn't say bad things about other players or brag about his own skills—he doesn't need to. He simply expresses an attitude that comes from high drummer self-esteem. Traits of aggressiveness and cockiness can sometimes be off-putting, and not everyone has a personality like Ben's. But at the very least you want to develop a core of confidence in yourself and have an outward display of assertiveness when dealing with others in the world of music.

Before I show you some ways to develop high drummer self-esteem, I'm going to give a quick scratch to my Freudian beard and speculate about a period of time in your life that might have been the genesis of your feeling a lack of confidence.

Parental Introjections

An introjection is simply a message, attitude, or philosophy that your parents or other authority figures imparted to you when you were a child. You heard their words and then incorporated them into your way of operating in the world. Their words became your beliefs.

Some introjections were helpful, such as:

Look both ways before you cross the street.

Be kind to others.

Don't eat yellow snow.

Some introjections, however, weren't so helpful, or were downright wrong:

Poor people are lazy.

Don't trust anyone.

The world is a cruel place.

Then there are the introjections that were personally damaging to you:

You'll never amount to anything.

You're a bad boy.

I wish you were never born.

Those last three introjections can seep into every part of your being, skewing your overall worldview. In a specific sense, they infiltrate the part of you that's a drummer, diminishing, if not destroying, your belief in yourself.

You have a choice regarding the introjections that continue to damage you. You can believe them, burn them, or bury them. Should you choose options two or three, the methods for disposal are relatively easy. Here's how…

On a sheet of paper, write the introjection (e.g., "You're a loser and will never amount to anything"). In a safe place, light the paper on fire and watch that toxic message go up in smoke. Or tear up the sheet of paper and thrust the shreds deep into a trash can. Or dig a small hole in the ground and put the torn-up message to rest—forever.

New Introjections

It's never too late to begin programming yourself with new, positive, helpful introjections. It's as if the more mature person you are now is correcting the old, corrosive, erroneous introjections of the past.

When you begin to work with these exercises, they might seem too simplistic to have much of an effect. Please take it on faith that if you practice the exercises, they *will* work for you. Sometimes the best solutions are the simplest, and words are extremely powerful. They possess healing and curative abilities, and they can be the agents for lasting change.

To begin, stock up on some 3x5 index cards. For global reprogramming, write the following introjections:

I'm a likeable, lovable person.

Other people are no better than I am.

I have much to contribute to this world.

For drumming-specific introjections, try these:

For whatever the reason, drums found me.

My skills continue to improve with each practice session.

I'm proud of each of my accomplishments, no matter how big or small.

I deserve to do well with my drumming.

I am worthy enough to play with confidence and joy in my heart.

Read these messages and absorb the words into your heart. Reread them whenever you have a little free time, like while you're watching a ball game, eating breakfast, or waiting for your computer to boot up. The entire process should take less than a minute. Eventually you'll memorize the introjections, and they'll become an integral part of your belief system.

You can also purchase a handheld audio recorder and record your introjections on it. Play the recordings at night, just before you fall asleep. Trust that they will sink deeply into your unconscious mind. Over time, you'll begin to notice a change in your thoughts, feelings, and actions, and you'll find that your drummer self-confidence is growing.

If you decide to record your introjections, use a voice that's rich with passion, strength, and confidence.

Physiology/Body Countenance/Posture

Want to make yourself depressed and bummed out? It's very simple to do. Just slump your shoulders and drop all expression from your face. (Do not smile.) Drop your head so that your chin is touching your chest, and stare at the ground. Now walk around shuffling your feet, with your arms hanging limp at your side. Inside your head, tell yourself things like: "It's no use. I never catch a break. Nobody likes me. Life's a bummer, and there's nothing I can do about it." How do you feel? Down? Sadly, far too many people trudge through life this way.

Why did this simple posture work? You were able to make yourself feel bad (kinesthetic) because you positioned your body in the physiology of someone who's depressed and despondent. Your body communicated these feelings to your head, and you gave your state of despair a little boost by adding some negative self-talk (audio) to seal the deal.

Want to reverse the process and put yourself in a positive, upbeat state? Again, it's very simple. Relax and let your shoulders drop comfortably. Smile naturally. Hold your head up high, with your chin slightly upward. Repeat a chain of internal statements like, "Life is good. I have many opportunities for growth and success. I love to play, and I'm a good drummer!" Stand up tall, straighten your back, and walk with a confident stride, arms swinging relaxed and loose at your sides.

I've seen drummers shamble up to the stage holding a rag-doll posture. Unless your band is going to perform music that's very dark, or you're playing a funeral dirge, positioning your body in this way can be dangerous to your drummer self-esteem. There's nothing uplifting, physically or emotionally, about this physiology. In the December 2007 of *Modern Drummer*, which is a tribute to the bebop pioneer Max Roach, jazz great Billy Drummond says, "The first time I saw Max, what struck me was the way he carried himself. He was confident, proud—but not in an arrogant way. A positive, strong way." See how posture can make all the difference?

A genuine smile is also important to drummer self-esteem, and it often starts with positive mental images. These thoughts may be on a preconscious or unconscious level. Here's how to bring the thoughts to a more conscious level, should you find yourself smiling while drumming. Simply ask yourself, "Why am I smiling?" Your responses should be on the order of statements like:

"It feels good to be drumming, like my whole body is glowing."

"People are really diggin' the music!"

"This feels effortless, and it sounds great!"

There are many drummers who play with a genuine, natural smile, and watching them perform makes me want to smile, too. The great smiling drummers include Walfredo Reyes Jr., Carter Beauford, Shawn Pelton, Chad Smith, Billy Higgins, Joey Baron, and Steve Smith, plus percussionists Raul Rekow and Alex Acuña. A true in-performance smile communicates, "I'm happy to be alive and happy to be here. I'm loving my drumming and am ecstatic that I can share my energy and gift with you."

Cognitions

All of the strategies for building drummer-specific self-esteem involve action. In other words, you have to *do something* within your thoughts and/or behaviors.

It's been estimated that over the course of a day, 60,000 thoughts run through the mind. If that's the case, you should:

1. Focus on the helpful ones that simply show up in your awareness.
2. Construct thoughts that will be beneficial in some way.
3. Diminish or delete thoughts that weaken positive self-esteem.

Let's construct some thoughts that will be of benefit. Begin by finding a quiet, comfortable place to sit or lie down. Close your eyes and imagine that you're in a movie theater and you're the only member of the audience. You've got the best seat in the house, and your view of the screen is clear and unobstructed. On the screen, place all of your past positive drumming experiences. (If you're a beginner and have yet to play drums in public, place a picture or movie of a good lesson or practice session on the screen.) Maybe these experiences show up on the screen as still prints or photos, or maybe the images play like movie footage that has been spliced together from various takes. Whenever possible, see the images in color. If it's a situation where the colors are bold and bright, really make them pop.

Now add the dimension of sound. Hear your drumming coming from state-of-the-art speakers on both sides of the screen. Each component in your kit speaks clearly and distinctly in its own voice. Watch yourself interact with your bandmates. Perhaps you're smiling. Finally, allow yourself to feel the sensations connected to watching and hearing your drumming at its finest. What would you label these emotions? Confidence? Joy? Excitement? Pleasure? Whatever it is, feel it and enjoy the moment.

After reliving some of your peak drumming experiences from your theater seat, imagine standing up, walking to the screen, and stepping into the scene. In your mind, put yourself there once again. It doesn't matter if the image is a movie or a photo; just step into it. Look out and see what you see, hear what you hear, and feel what you feel. First, notice the sensations on the outside of your body—the sticks in your hands, your throne supporting you, your feet moving on the pedals. Now go inward and feel all the wonderful sensations that you experience when you're creating music through your instrument. Stay there for a few moments, basking in the glow of your accomplishments, and then slowly open your eyes.

You've just learned a technique for building drummer self-esteem using past experiences. You can also imagine positive experiences in the future. (This is almost identical to the "success video" I had you construct in Chapter 1. The difference is that we'll go a little slower so that you can learn a more complete, comprehensive version of the technique.)

The recipe remains essentially the same.

1. Start in a quiet, comfortable place. Eyes closed.

2. Imagine yourself in a movie theater.

3. Cast onto the screen a scene in the *future* where you're playing at your best. Whether you see a movie or a photo, the format doesn't matter.

4. Allow yourself to experience all the wonderful feelings associated with this image.

5. After a while, imagine stepping into the picture, as if you're actually there and looking out with your own two eyes. Make sure you create sound and sensations. Hear your drums by themselves or in the context of a band. Feel sensations on the outside first—hands holding sticks, feet on pedals—and then feel the emotions on the inside—confidence, competence, power, joy, excitement, and so on.

6. Savor the experience. When you're ready, open your eyes and welcome yourself back into the here and now.

Whether you recall memorable drum experiences from the past or invent ones for the future, the most important step is when you step into the pictures. That's when you're most closely associated with the scene, and the emotions are much stronger.

Let's move on to diminishing or deleting those thoughts or memories that have hindered your drumming self-esteem. Start once again by finding a quiet, comfortable place where you won't be disturbed or distracted. (Turn off your cell phone.) Ease into a chair or lie on your bed. Close your eyes. In the theater of your mind, picture an old 12" or 13" black-and-white television that has just a few channels. Make a fuzzy but recognizable picture appear on the screen of a negative drumming experience from your past. It could be a gig where you couldn't seem to nail anything, or a time when someone made a disparaging remark about your playing. Look at the image, recognize it, and then let the screen fade to black. Gone.

Notice how you feel. Better?

If you want to dig deeper, reach out and change the channel on the TV to bring up another memory that, when it comes into view, takes away from your drummer self-esteem. See it, recognize it, and then let the image fade to black.

Should there be visuals from your childhood that you believe are toxic to your feeling your best, switch the channel to that memory. See it, recognize it, and then let the image fade to a completely black, dead screen.

When you feel as though you've done enough work for this session, simply open your eyes, and you're back in the here and now. It takes courage to face these images, and I commend you for taking on the challenge.

I'll end this chapter with a story that might hold special significance for you.

Legend has it that when man was created, the angels were jealous because man was given courage derived from the divine spark. Because of their envy, the angels conspired to conceal this knowledge from man. They began to search for a hiding place.

One angel suggested, "Hide it in the sky."

Another said, "Let's bury it deep in the earth."

Still another offered, "We'll cast it deep into the sea."

But the wisest of all the angels said, "No, we'll hide it in the heart of man himself. He'll never think of looking for it there."

Chapter 4: Setting Goals

Why should you set goals? Because if you don't have a written set of goals, you'll be prone to be blown through life sideways. And if you don't know where you're going and you fail to set a course for yourself, you may eventually wind up someplace you never wanted to be!

Establishing concrete goals will clearly point out the direction you need to take and will help get you what you want from your relationships with drumming, music, and life.

To illustrate the process of goal setting—or lack thereof—here are histories of two of my good friends from high school. Kevin was very goal oriented and focused on his future. Even though the rest of my friends in the 1960s didn't write down their goals, Kevin did. He kept a little notebook, and in it he'd listed his goals, his strategies for achieving them, and any possible obstacles. It read something like this:

1. Become a lawyer.
2. Make a lot of money.
3. Buy a big house.
4. Learn how to play golf.
5. Get married (after becoming a lawyer).
6. Have a couple kids.
7. Retire early.

Kevin laid the groundwork for acceptance into law school by getting top grades in high school. He then attended and graduated from law school, made a lot of cash in his career, bought a big house, and retired at age fifty. As he'd written years before, he held off on getting married until he had passed the bar exam. He feared that marriage, and the possibility of having children, might distract him from his studies while in school. Unfortunately, this strategy conflicted with his long-term girlfriend's wishes. She refused to wait for a wedding and eventually walked out. After Kevin became a practicing attorney, he did marry—twice. Both times the nuptials ended in divorce. He did have children, one with each wife. And he did learn the game of golf.

As you can see, Kevin's life isn't perfect. To quote Rolling Stones singer Mick Jagger: "You can't always get what you want." But in terms of goals, Kevin achieved six out of seven. I'm not sure why he's been so unlucky in love; maybe the institution of marriage just isn't for him. But he talks with pride and passion about many of the challenging cases he'd worked on over the years. He retired early because he chose a profession that paid well. In warm weather, he enjoys playing golf and socializing with other golfers who have also retired early. Kevin recently bought himself a lap steel guitar and is taking lessons, freely admitting that if the instrument doesn't continue to provide entertainment or a sense of fun, he'll abandon it and try something else. He has grandchildren and enjoys spending time with them. Kevin has labeled himself as happy.

Although he was very bright, my other friend Chris was a goof-off in high school—the classic underachiever. When asked what he wanted to do after graduation, he always responded, "Party and have a good time." He attended college, although it took him six years to complete a four-year program in liberal arts. His degree was so general that he wasn't qualified for many jobs upon graduation. He wanted the same things as the rest of us who were in our early twenties—a nice apartment or house, a girlfriend or wife, maybe a kid or two, a little money, and a hobby or pastime. Chris easily found an entry-level, low-paying job with the state of New York—a day gig that consisted of affixing numbers to the back of state property (typewriters, furniture, filing cabinets, etc.). He was able to afford a decent apartment, eventually got married, and had some discretionary funds. He's still employed by the state of New York, although he's admitted he's never felt fulfilled.

Job-wise, Chris is the perfect example of someone who's been "blown sideways through life." For more than thirty years, he's gone to work simply because he's needed a paycheck. He admits there has never been any real fulfillment, passion, or joy with his job. Chris is married and has one child, but he never cultivated any hobbies or pastimes. When at home, he watches endless TV (whatever catches his interest at that moment), while drinking beer and eating junk food. He'll occasionally push himself off the couch to attend one of his son's baseball games. Chris has admitted to feeling restless on the weekends, but when he looks for something to do he often resorts to grabbing the TV remote and a bag of chips.

As we can see from those two examples, there's no clear-cut path to success or fulfillment, but we seem to be better off when we have a specific set of goals.

When writing your own goals, try to make them as precise as possible. What do you want from drumming and your life? Once again, it's time to be completely honest with yourself. Do some very deep soul-searching. Would you like to be a full-time musician, or will gigging on the weekends be enough to fulfill your needs? Looking at other aspects of your life, what do you want in a romantic relationship? Would you like children? How about hobbies and pastimes? (I'm hitting this topic from the standpoint of someone who has just completed high school or college, but if you've already established a "grown-up" life for yourself, this is the time to question where you are and where you *want* to be.)

Are you happy? Do you feel fulfilled? Does the current state of your musical and/or personal life offer maximum enjoyment and satisfaction? If not, think long and hard about these questions, decide what's working (or perhaps what isn't working), and begin to make changes accordingly. Notice I said to *begin* to make changes accordingly. I'm not suggesting that you revamp your life overnight. But if change is what you want and need, start where you've pinpointed a deficit, and modify your behaviors at your own rate and pace. Keep in mind that whatever you decide to change might impact those closest to you, and their reactions may not always be supportive.

Earlier in the book I introduced you to the work-love-play model. Let's apply it here, too.

Work

If you're already working as a full-time drummer, are you getting what you need out of your career? Are you fulfilled by the type of music you're playing, the financial compensation for your hard work, your bandmates' company, and the overall lifestyle of being a full-time musician? If you're on tour, does the travel aspect of your profession satisfy you?

If you're a part-time professional drummer, is it enough? Also ask yourself the same questions listed above. For many drummers, part-time work is all we need to feel fulfilled. It gives us exactly what we want from a musical situation, and it fulfills our need for a creative, performance-oriented outlet. If you aren't satisfied just gigging on the weekends, how would you go about making a bid to become a full-time drummer? And are you willing to sacrifice certain comforts in your life in order to make that leap?

Love

Unless we're part of a religious sect that forbids marriage, most of us couple up with a life partner. Perhaps it's part of our anthropological make-up that causes us humans to fall into a state called love and form some sort of long-term commitment to another person. Romantic love is a mysterious state that I'm not about to explore here. But when you first meet this other person who eventually becomes your significant other, it's often difficult—if not impossible—to put the raging hormones and dreamy thoughts aside so you can determine whether he or she truly meshes with your goals in life. Perhaps that's why the divorce rate is so high these days. As you embark on your journey toward love, keep in mind that not everyone will be as in tune with art, music, and drumming as you are. If your primary goal is to become a full- or part-time professional drummer, it's important to find someone who supports that decision and understands that sacrifices are involved in pursuing such a lifestyle.

Play

Recreation is important. You need to unwind and change up your normal day-to-day routine. The old maxim, "All work and no play makes Jack a dull boy," is true. And you want to engage in an activity that doesn't necessarily have a tangible outcome. Picture a child finger painting. As adults, we've been socialized to be outcome oriented, so we might ask this child, "What are you making?" The child might respond, "Nothing, I'm just painting." The child merely enjoys the process of slathering paint on glossy paper. That's all there is to it, and that's all it should be. There's a lesson to be learned here: Enjoy the process, not the outcome.

To fulfill your needs for play, you might want to try some type of physical exercise. If you like to run, then go for a simple jog, but don't get hung up on trying to break a six-minute mile. Just enjoy the process. Some people like to collect things—paintings, books, sculpture, antique toys, or drums. Traveling, dining out, and visiting museums are all hobbies many people have adopted to break from their typical daily routines. The key is that the activity should carry a primary element of enjoyment and not necessarily accomplishment.

I'm going to invent a character; we'll call him Bob. Bob is in his late thirties, is happily married, has a son, and finds his work as a technical writer very rewarding. Bob is also a drummer and has recently been starting to question where drums fit into his life.

Bob played in a variety of bands while in high school and college. But since his mid-twenties, Bob has placed drumming in the realm of "play." About three times a week after work, he'll go out to his drumset in the garage, put on his headphones, and groove along to some tunes on his MP3 player. His family knows that this is Bob's way to relax after work, and they don't disturb him. He usually plays for thirty to forty-five minutes.

When Bob and his wife recently attended a wedding, there was a five-piece band playing at the reception. Bob began daydreaming about what it would be like to perform again. The thought stayed with him, and while drumming in the garage the next day, he began to fantasize about playing for an audience. Afterward, he got out a notebook and a pen and wrote the following goals:

Work: Solid for now, but shoot for a managerial position within the next three years. A supervisor has talked about retiring, so there's a possible opening there.

Love: Try to attend more of Scotty's soccer games. If I feel too tired to go, have a cup of coffee or an energy drink. Scotty always looks disappointed when I don't go. He won't be a kid forever. I should start going...I want to start going more often.

Play: Investigate the possibility of joining or starting a wedding/party band. I miss playing out! Fridays and/or Saturdays only, and no more than one or two practices per week.

Fast-forward a couple weeks. Bob got the okay from his wife to look into joining a band. In a local arts and entertainment newspaper, Bob connected with a working band seeking a drummer. He auditioned and got the gig. After learning the repertoire, Bob is now scheduled to be out most Saturday afternoons or evenings performing with his new band.

Now eight months have passed. Learning his new band's repertoire took more time and effort than Bob had anticipated. Because he had to spend more time practicing at home, Bob actually attended *fewer* of his son's games. His son appeared angry and hurt, and Bob feels that Scotty has distanced himself. Bob's wife wound up having to do most of the yard work and weekend chores while he was off playing with his band. Lately, Bob has had back-to-back gigs on Saturdays, playing in the afternoon and in the evening. His wife has begun to distance herself as well. Bob, however, has been having a blast, and the extra cash he's made from gigging has helped with the overall family income.

What's to be learned here? Many times, change comes with a price. When you live in a family unit, a change in your behavior affects others—positively, negatively, or both.

Here are some possible solutions for Bob's situation.

Bob needs to call a family meeting where he discusses his drumming. Now that he's learned his band's repertoire, he most likely won't have to practice as much and will have more time to spend with his family. Bob also needs to work out a schedule so there's a more equal division of household labor between him and his wife.

Bob also needs to stress to his son and his wife how much he enjoys drumming and how fulfilling it is to be playing with a band again. But if his current band is playing too often and is causing a strained relationship with both his wife and son, Bob might have to look for a group with a gigging schedule that's a little lighter, or he'll have to deal with a period of feeling fatigued while he juggles his gig schedule with attending more of his son's games and splitting chores with his wife. Either way, he'll have to make a sacrifice in order to find a balance between his family life and his new drumming career.

Here's another illustration of the use of—and sometimes the fallout from—setting goals.

Levon is the drummer for an alt-country band, the Loan Arrangers, that has built a good-size following in western Massachusetts. The band plays at least two times a week, often traveling across the state for gigs in Boston. The group's merch tent has been doing quite well with sales of the Arrangers' self-produced CDs, T-shirts, and hats. Levon has a day job as a recording engineer at a small studio where he primarily records jingles and voice-overs. His boss allows for a flexible schedule to accommodate the band, as long as the recording work gets done.

Levon's wife, Laura, is a batik artist. The two met in college. Both are in their late twenties and have no children. Although Levon works in a studio and often gets the nod to drum on jingles and other sessions, he spends most of his time fantasizing about making it big with his band.

One night, Levon decides to type out his goals on his laptop:

Work: Within the next year, I want to leave the recording studio and tour with the Loan Arrangers. My goal is for the band to get noticed and signed by a major label. I would like to leave the door open at the studio, however, should I need to return to work there. I will spend every available hour planning the minute details of the tour and see if we can get a sponsor.

Love: I need to pitch the concept of the tour to Laura to see if she's cool with it and also with my dipping into our savings if money gets tight on the road.

Play: I want to start meditating and jogging again.

Within a year, Levon and his band did embark on an East Coast tour. His boss at the studio was less than happy that Levon made no provisions for finding someone to replace him, although this was never discussed. Laura was excited and totally supportive about Levon's decision to go for the big time. Her stipulation regarding their savings was that she'd wire Levon money if he needed it, knowing her husband's propensity for spending cash a little too freely.

Unfortunately, not once during the tour did a representative from a major record label approach the band, so when the tour ended Levon returned to Massachusetts and took a day job at a music store. (His old boss refused to hire him back.) The band is now working on its second album, and Levon is working on a new set of goals, which includes landing a manager or booking agent.

Both Bob and Levon achieved most of what they wanted. Although Levon's band didn't connect with a major label, Levon was able to tour, and his group garnered some additional exposure to a wider audience.

Personalities play a part in goal setting and implementation. Levon and Laura are artists, which perhaps makes them more inclined to realize the risks and sacrifices inherent to the creative arts. Bob's wife has more traditional family values, so the big change she saw was an absent husband when work needed to be done.

The bottom line is that you should always write down your specific goals. This will concretize and give direction to your wishes and desires. Keep in mind that unless you live alone and have absolutely no attachments or responsibilities, the implementation of your goals will most likely impact those around you—for better or for worse.

Chapter 5: Conflict

"Hell is other people." —*from* No Exit *by Jean-Paul Sartre*

I won't go as far as philosopher Sartre, but let's just say that interpersonal relationships can be challenging. Others have different ideas, beliefs, opinions, values, and notions that don't always agree with your way of seeing and functioning in the world. So what happens when you don't meet eye to eye with another person? Often the result is conflict.

Michael Flatley, world-class dancer, choreographer, and originator of *Riverdance*, was once asked during an interview if there was anything that surprised him after he had achieved fame and fortune. He answered something to the effect that with his hard-won celebrity status, he expected it to be devoid of conflict. He said he was shocked when his days did include conflict. After his initial disappointment, he adopted an attitude of embracing conflict—not seeking it out, but knowing that each and every day would include at least one conflict to overcome.

Drummers are constantly interacting with others—bandmates, family members, friends, fans, club owners, and so on. There's bound to be conflict with someone at some point.

So where's the mental barrier here? It's embedded in the fact that if you don't handle conflict well, you're apt to retreat from the situation, perhaps even to the point where you shrink away from your career completely, especially if drumming is involved in the conflict.

I'm going to offer some conflict scenarios, as well as suggestions for how to deal with them. Before I lay these out, here are a few tips to remember when you're attempting to resolve a conflict.

1. Try to put any hot emotions aside. Take a couple deep breaths or take a walk to cool down before you approach the other person. Don't use alcohol or any other intoxicant to calm yourself down—or to build up your courage—before a confrontation. Think with a cool and clear head.

2. Once you start expressing your concerns, make "I" statements that

demonstrate that you own a thought or belief. Avoid accusations, name calling, and generalizations. Keep your communications clear, to the point, concrete, and simple.

3. Whenever possible, don't have an audience when attempting to resolve a conflict. Any type of outside observer watching your interaction, whether it's one or one hundred people, will drastically change the dynamics, and usually for the worse.

4. Attempt to keep your complaints and issues to a maximum of three topics. Any more than that, and the other person starts to become mentally overwhelmed and emotions can become heated.

5. Practice a matter-of-fact demeanor. If you assert yourself with a menacing sneer, that's usually all the other person sees and focuses on. He or she hears nothing of your attempts at resolution.

NLP (Neuro-Linguistic Programming, from which the VAK model is derived) can also be a tool to sharpen your communication skills and gain insight into the way individuals tend to learn and encode information they receive about the world. Listen closely the next time you have a conversation with a friend or associate. You might hear:

"I see what you're saying." This indicates a person who tends to be a visual learner and encodes his or her world primarily in pictures and internal movies.

"I wouldn't hear of such a thing!" This person is likely an audio learner/encoder/communicator.

"Yeah, that feels right." A comment like this would come from a kinesthetic learner who expresses himself or herself from a feeling level.

These aren't absolutes, as all of us are apt to mix and match the three modalities. When communicating with another person, zoom in on the words the other person favors, and identify whether that person tends to be visual, auditory, or kinesthetic. Then tailor your words to match that sense. NLP theory purports that you will have a better rapport with others (and you'll exert more influence) because you're literally "speaking their language."

Okay, it's time for our first fictional conflict scenario.

Picture this: It's the middle of summer, but it's way below zero in your household. Even your twin nine-year-old sons have been asking why you and Mommy are fighting so much.

You're the drummer in a heavy metal band, and you recently had your first tattoo inked into the length of your arm. You've been talking about getting the tattoo for several months. You love it, but your wife appears furious. A week has passed, and she's barely spoken a word to you. At times you've even noticed that her eyes have been red from crying. When you ask what's wrong, she responds (coldly), "Nothing."

You love your wife, you've had a good marriage to this point, and you want this conflict to end. Here's what you could try. First, get the kids out of the house. Send them out on a playdate with some friends, or drop them off at your parents' house for a couple hours. Again, this is one time when you don't want an audience.

> You: "When I look at you, you seem angry at me."
> Her (tears start to flow): "I'm not angry. I'm scared."
> You: "Scared? Scared of what?"
> Her: "That you've become a drug addict."
> You: "What? You know I don't do drugs—never have and never will."
> Her: "But a couple of the guys in your band have tattoos, and they do drugs."
> You: "That's them, and that's their business. I got the tattoo because I always wanted one."
> Her (sighs): "So you're not doing drugs?"
> You: "No! I got the tattoo because I liked the design, and it has special meaning to me. I'd like to tell you about it, if you'd let me."
> Her: "Okay, maybe... But I still don't like it."
> You: "And maybe you never will, but there's no reason to worry."
> Your wife smiles and nods, and you hug one another.

Let's analyze this scenario. Your wife was an unfortunate victim of what I call junk-o logic. In this case, her thought was that all men who have tattoos use drugs. Where's the evidence to support that? It doesn't exist. You were guilty by association because a couple of your bandmates with tattoos use drugs. Notice that both parties used "I" statements to own their thoughts and feelings, kept a cool head, and avoided name calling. A statement like "Only an idiot would think that way" could have ruined what eventually was a positive outcome. Plus the encounter was focused on one topic only.

Here's a second imaginary conflict scenario.

You join a blues trio. Although you don't perceive yourself as strictly a blues drummer, you enjoy the music, your bandmates, the gigs, and the extra cash. The leader, who's the singer and guitarist in the band, is deep into blues culture. He knows the history of the music, collects old blues LPs, goes to see name bluesmen when they're playing locally, and considers himself a purist. Blues music is his life.

Like you, the bass player thinks of himself as a musician who plays in a blues band. He's not strictly a blues bassist. He's quiet, does his job, and collects his pay at the end of the night. He never ruffles any feathers.

Although the leader occasionally compliments your playing, he often mentions during rehearsals that he wants you to listen to blues CDs to hear some "real" blues drummers. You assert yourself, stating that you think of yourself as a drummer who plays a variety of styles, but you don't show any enthusiasm when he offers to let you borrow some CDs.

One night on a gig, you slip a China cymbal into your setup. Throughout the night, when you think the China would add a different hue to your palette of sonic colors, you play it. Each time you do, the leader gives you a curious look.

Another night, you substitute a splash in place of a more conventional crash cymbal. You begin a song in the second set by hitting the splash, and you receive an ugly glare from the bandleader. During load-out, you assert yourself to the bandleader.

You (scowling): "Dude, what was with that look during the second set?"

Leader (sarcastically): "What was with that little toy cymbal?"

You (defensively): "It's called a splash, and it's not a toy."

Leader (voice rising in anger): "Yeah, well, the only splashing I want to hear would be if I was swimming."

You: "So you don't like the sound?"

Leader: "Never heard it played in the blues. In fact, it's disrespectful to play the blues that way."

You: "You're crazy!"

Leader: "And you're fired."

What went wrong here? First, it seems the bandleader wanted a "real" blues drummer all along. He wasn't honest with himself, and he wasn't honest with you. His true desire to sound completely authentic was always lurking in the background, even though he sometimes complimented you on your drumming.

Your choice of cymbals was just the tip of the iceberg regarding the true underlying problem in this shaky working relationship. You were asserting some simple artistic choices, but he saw it as not playing in the blues tradition. The actual root of the problem was that you refused to identify yourself as a bluesman. You were clear and consistent in stating your diverse tastes in music and drumming styles. This frustrated the bandleader and perhaps put him on the path of looking for a way to create a conflict between you two.

There were a number of strong negative emotions running red hot during the confrontation. You initiated the interaction with the word *dude*, which in this situation wasn't the best choice, because it carried a negative connotation. Sarcasm and name calling also threw gas on the fire.

In retrospect, if the leader truly wanted a more authentic blues drummer, he should have hired one. And if your gut was telling you that he really wasn't happy with your style, you might have been better off looking for a different band. Although you verbalized that you're a drummer who plays a variety of styles, you never verbalized specifically that you didn't want to be pigeonholed as strictly a blues drummer.

There are a few things that you could have done to steer your interaction in another direction, to either avoid or resolve the conflict before it escalated. First, you could have looked the bandleader straight in the eye and asked if he'd be happier with a drummer who's more of a traditional blues player. (The eye contact is essential, and, again, no audience! This includes the bass player, spouses, kids, etc.) If he said yes, you could have been a stand-up guy and offered to help him look for one or let him know you'd stay on until he found someone else.

To avoid the confrontation entirely, you could have insisted on borrowing some blues CDs from the leader at the end of your rehearsals. This shows that you're taking a more active interest in the music, even if you don't decide to completely overhaul your playing style to become a more traditional blues player.

When you swapped out cymbals during the gig and got the ugly looks, you could have questioned the leader after the gig with a more matter-of-fact tone. Even when he said things about how those types of cymbals have never been played in the blues, you could have maintained a flat affect and given him a light apology. That likely would have avoided the angry exchange, and you would have retained your place in the band.

The major question to ask yourself: How much do I want this gig? If you have four kids at home and an estranged wife who recently split to take up with a singer in a death metal band, and you just lost your day job, well, maybe you need to be a bit more accommodating, at least until the chaos in your life is sorted out. But if you're just playing in this band for fun, determine if it's really worth the extra effort to keep things cool between you and your bandleader.

One last thought about this scenario, and then we'll move on to the final example of handling conflict. Humor can be very effective for de-escalating things when trouble is brewing. For example, when the bandleader made a crack about the "toy" splash cymbal, you could have smiled and said, "Hey, I paid a hundred bucks for that toy. But if you don't think it fits, I won't use it."

A smile often defuses a potentially explosive situation. You may be ingratiating yourself a bit, but if you want to keep the gig….

In this final conflict scenario, not only are you the drummer in a band but you're also the leader. You've been gigging at Uncle Bucky's Chuckle Hut, a local bar, restaurant, and comedy club. Before your band plays three sets, you provide intro and outro music for amateur comics, plus the occasional rimshot and cymbal choke on cue.

The crowd often consists of a small number of loyal patrons who are usually in a good mood by the time your band comes on, having been warmed up by the comics. You've performed about half a dozen gigs at Uncle Bucky's. It's a nice place, the bathrooms are relatively clean, the owner (Bucky) is friendly, and he peels off your cash without question at the end of the night. It's a comfortable environment for your five-piece band.

Unfortunately, an economic recession begins to erode Bucky's business. The customers start to thin out, and Bucky mentions to you, in general terms, the idea of making a change in an attempt to survive. One night when you're scheduled to play, you walk in and a DJ is setting up. You speculate that this must be the change Bucky was talking about. There are also no comedians anywhere to be found. The DJ gives you a cursory glance that sends out an aura of arrogance. Your female lead singer asks him what time he'll be starting, and the guy replies, "Talk to Bucky." You spy Bucky behind the bar, looking wide-eyed and nervous. As the bandleader, it's your job to find out what's going on, so you approach Bucky.

Bucky confirms that the comedians are out and the DJ is in—for the *entire* night. Bucky explains that this DJ has an excellent following but is somewhat irresponsible when it comes to showing up on time, so he deliberately double booked, for fear of having no entertainment on a Saturday night. Your band was hired as back-up. You keep your cool.

When you return to your bandmates and explain the situation, each person has a different reaction. The bass player wants to punch Bucky in the face. The female singer wants to scream obscenities at Bucky and the DJ. The lead guitarist slips into a temporary catatonic state. And the keyboardist confronts the DJ, who responds, "Your gripe is with Bucky, not me. I didn't ask to come here. It's just another gig in some dump."

As a bandleader, it's your job to attempt to resolve this situation in a civil and nonviolent manner. Here's a possible way to do so:

After asking to talk to Bucky in a back room (no audience), you look him in the eye and request your full pay for the evening, informing him—with a matter-of-fact demeanor—that what he did was unprofessional. No drama. You are simply making a direct request. Bucky claims he's behind in his bills and hopes that the DJ will pull enough of a crowd tonight to help him bail out of his financial woes. Bucky claims he can't pay you anything other than gas money. You counter by saying that in fairness the members of the band should at least receive a food/drink certificate for the amount they would have made that evening. Bucky agrees. You get the gas money in cash, and Bucky scribbles out five gift certificates.

Although your lead singer loudly proclaims that she's going to slander Bucky on Craigslist as a slacker and the keyboardist threatens to destroy the club's stage lighting, your band takes the gas money and gift certificates and departs.

Two weeks later, Bucky's club is closed for good, and he's working at a local dry cleaner's. The gift certificates are now worthless. Even though you and your bandmates ended up getting the short end of the deal, no one caused too much trouble the night of the double booking. As bandleader, you handled this conflict well, free meal or no free meal.

What's to be learned from this situation? The entertainment trade is a fickle, unpredictable, exciting, and glorious business. In order to maintain your sanity, you'll have to learn to deal with conflicts when they arise. Sure, violence and bully tactics can be used to get what you want, but I'm recommending assertiveness, standing your ground, communicating truthfully, and trying to coax honesty out of the other person.

I'll end this chapter with a story.

A mother snake and her child take up residence near a school. One day the mother snake comes home and finds several children crying and holding bleeding snakebites inflicted by the baby snake.

"What happened?" the mother snake asks her child.

"They made fun of me, so I bit them," says the baby snake proudly.

"Oh, no, you must never do that again," the mother snake says. "To inflict violence and pain is bad." The baby snake hangs its head in shame, and the mother's admonishment of her offspring does not go unnoticed by the children who are still nursing their wounds.

The following day, the mother snake comes home to find the baby snake all bloody and battered.

"What happened?" she cries.

"The children beat me up on their way to school," says the baby snake with little reptile tears leaking from its eyes.

"Why didn't you defend yourself?" asks the mother snake.

"Because you told me not to bite them."

The mother snake pauses. "Yes, I told you not to bite or hurt them," she says wisely. "But I never said you couldn't *hiss*!"

Chapter 6: Anxiety, Fear, And Stress

Anxiety has been called the affliction of the "what ifs." Here are a few examples that may have terrorized you in the past (or maybe still do):

"What if I blow that fill I've been struggling with in practice?"

"What if my timing is off again tonight?"

"What if I drop a stick?"

"What if the spring on my kick pedal breaks?"

"What if my solo stinks and the crowd boos."

"What if my throne tips over?"

"What if? What if? *What if?*"

These types of anxiety-producing thoughts are endless. When you're in a performance situation and you feel excessively tense, you're experiencing what's called performance anxiety or stage fright.

Anyone can suffer from stage fright, including big-name drummers who have to play every night for thousands of fans. Here's an example from the May 2006 issue of *Modern Drummer*, where Foo Fighters drummer Taylor Hawkins discusses his battles with performance anxiety.

MD: I understand you suffer from stage fright.

Taylor: I still do; it's awful. There are nights when I don't feel comfortable. It's like I'm fighting the whole night. Thankfully, most of the time nobody can tell. I'll come off stage feeling awful and Dave [Grohl] will say, "I don't know what you're talking about. You sounded great." It's just because I don't feel comfortable. I love playing the drums, and I play all the time. But I do suffer serious stage fright. Nothing helps. I warm up, take deep breaths.

In the March 2007 issue of *Modern Drummer*, Elton John drummer Nigel Olsson comments on his stage fright/performance anxiety issues: "I'm nervous every time I go on stage. I shake before I go on. But once I get up there, I'm fine."

Nigel's experience mirrors the progression—and subsequent dissolution—of my own stage nerves. Once I'm behind the kit, I feel at home and can relax…somewhat. After the first couple of songs, I'm immersed in the music and sinking into the fun of playing drums. My anxiety dissipates and is replaced with excitement and my belief that I'm contributing what I have to offer to the band, to our audience, and to the universe of music.

Performance anxiety can start days, weeks, or even months before the actual event. Think of all the time and energy you've wasted inventing these thoughts in your head. And that's just what they are: invented ideas from your wonderful, creative mind.

Stimulating sensations within your body are normal prior to performing. You're excited about sharing your music with the audience. But when this arousal crosses over into the red zone, it's no fun. Shaking, shivering, tight muscles, clammy hands, racing negative thoughts of disaster, dry mouth, stuttering, feeling as if you want to run away, dizziness, and nausea are all symptoms of high anxiety.

If you want to see an excellent depiction of performance anxiety, rent the movie *The Man With The Golden Arm*, starring Frank Sinatra. Sinatra's character is a drummer with a drug addiction, and there's a scene where he auditions for a band. In that scene, you'll see one of the worst physical cases of stage anxiety you can imagine.

Now let's bring in the VAK model when dealing with anxiety. Are your thoughts of something bad happening on stage coming to you in visual form? Are they pictures or movies? Or is it your internal self-talk that terrorizes you, feeding you catastrophic phrases that cause your palms to sweat, your heart to race, and your stomach to feel queasy? If so, that's the kinesthetic connection. Worse yet, are your thoughts of disaster on stage coming at you in both internal visual and auditory formats?

You can overcome the spectrum of stage fright—all the way from mild jitters to that all-encompassing feeling of dread that can ultimately cripple you and lead you to quit. I'm going to give you methods, strategies, and philosophies that are proven to be successful. Think of them in terms of trial and outcome. You may have to experiment with a number of the approaches until you find the ones that work for you.

There are three categories of methods for overcoming performance anxiety: mechanical, cognitive, and chemical. Let's examine each one.

Mechanical

Mechanical applies to anything that you do with your body to decrease anxiety. It coincides with the kinesthetic in VAK.

Any aerobic exercise, such as a brisk walk, an intense half hour on the elliptical machine at the gym, or mountain biking, will help to lessen your anxiety for the gig later that night. It will also assist greatly in building your cardiovascular stamina, which is very helpful due to the strenuous nature of drumming.

Weight training is also excellent for taming anxiety. You don't have to become a gym rat; just do a series of reps for your arms, legs, and core. (If you like hitting the gym, seek out a qualified trainer to help design some drummer-specific exercises for you.) Feeling stronger will help to lessen your anxiety. Be careful not to overdue it by lifting massive amounts of weight or by cranking out too many repetitions, or else you'll pay for it at the gig. You will have exhausted yourself and temporarily weakened the muscles you'll need to play well.

I incorporate many of the exercises demonstrated on Justin Spencer's DVD *Fitness For Drummers*. I also like to work out on a practice pad for ten to fifteen minutes a day, using heavy Power Wrist Builders metal sticks, before I sit down behind my kit for my formal practice. The heavy sticks both build and relax my muscles so that when I go back to regular wood sticks, they seem to swing a little easier. I've discovered that the stronger I feel—with good stamina and hand/arm/foot/leg strength—the more self-confidence I have on stage, and the less I'm prone to experience anxiety.

A few moments before showtime I might also perform a modified version of the Sarnoff Squeeze, which was created by the Broadway actress Dorothy Sarnoff. No special equipment is necessary; all you need is a wall. Sarnoff got the idea for this exercise after observing how actor Yul Brynner controlled his anxiety before performances of *The King And I* by simply pushing against a wall. Sarnoff devised a breathing method that runs contrary to the popular suggestion of taking some deep breaths when you're anxious.

Here's my version of Brynner and Sarnoff's techniques.

First, find a wall. I position myself about two feet from the wall and let my body fall toward it, catching myself with outstretched arms while I exhale all my breath. When I'm completely out of air, I push back away from the wall and let my lungs suck in air naturally. I exhale slowly and allow my shoulders to drop (not slouch) into a comfortable position. When your shoulders are raised, you assume a cowering position, as if there's something in your environment that is creating anxiety.

Taking a few deep breaths to calm yourself can actually do more harm than good. One or two slow, deep inhalations might help you to relax, but if you start sucking in huge gulps of air as if you're drowning, you might wind up dizzy or lightheaded because you're hyperventilating. Also, shallow breathing can make you feel anxious. Think of the last time you watched a horror movie. During the real scary parts you were breathing like a little bird—rapid and shallow. If your respiration is too fast and shallow, or if you hold your breath, your body goes into a state of alarm, believing that some threat is present. If you're feeling anxious, check your breathing. If it's short and shallow, deepen it by taking in a couple "belly breaths" (a breath where you see your stomach expand). If you find yourself holding your breath, especially when executing a quick or complex pattern on your drums, train yourself to breathe through it.

There are also some excellent electronic biofeedback tools that can help you to breathe in a way that will reduce anxiety. One that I've used is a small handheld device called an emWave, which paces your breathing with lights that run up and down a column. When your breathing is at the optimal depth and speed, a little bell sounds, giving you auditory feedback.

Progressive Muscle Relaxation

Many drummers find tense-and-release muscle relaxation exercises to be quite helpful. You can perform them on your own, and there are a number of CDs on the market that will walk you through the procedure. Usually the speaker on the CD guides you with a calm, soothing voice that's embedded in a background of soft music. You usually begin the technique either at your head or your feet. Tense the muscles, hold the tension for a few seconds, and then release. Some CDs get very specific about tensing and relaxing all the muscles in your body—like each individual finger—but if you simply hit the major muscle groups, working from top to bottom or bottom or top, the overall uptight feeling should leave you.

There are two problems associated with any of the tense-and-release progressive muscle relaxation techniques: time and place. You need to take your time when doing progressive muscle relaxation exercises. Many of the CDs require twenty minutes or more. Whether you're listening to a commercially produced CD with music or performing your own version, rushing through the process can diminish its effectiveness. Unless you get to the venue way ahead of time and you can find a quiet, private place to do the exercises, you likely won't have time to use this technique to relieve performance anxiety before the gig.

My suggestion is to perform the progressive tense-and-release muscle relaxation exercises before you leave for the gig. The comfort of your home or hotel room should give you the optimum peace and quiet you need. And if you perform the procedure about an hour or so before heading to the venue, you will still retain residual relaxation effects.

Another effective way to reduce anxiety mechanically is to take a hot shower or bath. This will further relax your muscles, and when your muscles (kinesthetic) send a message to your head (video and audio) that they're relaxed, this feedback loop reinforces that anxiety has been reduced.

Cognitive

To deal with stage fright on the cognitive level, you're working with your thoughts—your internal pictures and voices—to combat the emotion of anxiety.

There's a wealth of ways in which you can use cognitions to combat anxiety. We'll begin by using some of the principles associated with a way of functioning in the world known as rational-emotive. The concept holds that if you can train yourself to think more rationally, the magnitude of your negative emotions—in this case, anxiety—will be lessened.

I want to begin by sharing a real-life experience where irrational thought caused me some very painful anxiety. It was during the *Urban Cowboy* era (early 1980s), and country music was big. My band had a regular gig at a large venue that always drew a huge crowd. One night, I brought along a male friend to check out the band. (We'll call him Tom.) At the end of a song where I had a short solo, I caught a stick on the rim of a drum, which caused the stick to fly out of my hand. I was mortified. I thought for sure that everyone in the club saw and heard my mistake, and that they evaluated me as the world's worst drummer. This happened during the last song of the first set. When we went on break, I came off stage with my head hanging and shoulders slumped, and I was wishing there was a hole I could crawl into and hide. As I headed to the men's room, Tom walked up to me with a beer. "You guys sounded great," he said.

"Very funny," I replied, believing he was being facetious about my disastrous mistake.

"You didn't think so?" he questioned, frowning.

"C'mon. I made a total ass of myself on that last song. Stop pretending it didn't happen—you saw it!"

Tom looked down at the floor, then up at me. "See what?" He paused. "Uh, no offense, bro, but I couldn't keep my eyes off your lead singer. Man, she is amazing!"

There were three major errors in my thinking regarding this real-life incident. First, I assumed that all of the patrons in the club were giving me their total, undivided attention. (I call this mind reading.) I'm sure some people there caught my blunder, but I falsely assumed that they cared or in some way were evaluating me negatively. I had no evidence to support this and no way to validate my belief unless I wanted to ask each and every person in the club if they had seen me drop a stick.

The second error is what's known as catastrophizing. Cognitively, I made a mountain out of a molehill, but *nothing* bad ever came of my bungled fill. I wasn't fired, and no one in the band ever mentioned it, probably because they empathize with how embarrassing and uncomfortable it is to make a goof on stage.

The third error was overgeneralizing. I made one mistake in an entire set of otherwise well-played music, yet that's what I chose to focus on. That botched fill ruined my feelings about my abilities, and focusing on my mistake made my anxiety leak into every thought I had about that first set.

Before I give you instruction on how to combat negative thinking, it's important to understand that the engine that drives stage fright is a deep concern about negative evaluation. In other words, we fret—obsessively—about what others will think of us. Humans hate to be evaluated negatively; it remains one of our universal worries. But the reality is that most of us are so caught up in our own daily crises that we don't bother to look outside our somewhat narcissistic selves.

Okay, now for the way to combat irrational negative thinking about your drumming.

A-B-C-D-E

A represents the *activating* event. An example would be if you rushed a fill so badly that when you came back in with the beat, you had to adjust your playing in order to sync up with the rest of the band.

B stands for your *belief*—usually erroneous or irrational—about that event. In your mind, everyone in the audience evaluated you negatively for your mistake.

C is for the emotional *consequence* you feel because of your belief, which is always negative and often catastrophic. You may feel shame, self-loathing, or disgust, which turns on the internal self-talk about your being a lousy drummer.

D is when you go into action, *disputing* your original belief about the activating event. This action involves internal self-talk. Like the VAK model, you'll need to practice this. To yourself, say things like, "I'm human, and humans make mistakes," or, "It could have been worse; I could have frozen up and not finished the song at all." Or simply say, "So what." ("So what" shouldn't be taken as an indicator that you don't care about your drumming. It simply means that things like this happen to all of us.)

E is the first letter of *emotion*—the new emotional state that you've created by disputing the original erroneous/irrational belief. If you've done a good job of disputing the original belief, the positive result will be a change in your feeling about the activating event, which in this case was your onstage goof.

If you've been successful going through these methods, you might feel a bit embarrassed, chagrined, and somewhat humbled by your mistake. Maybe you weren't paying attention, and this experience teaches you to always stay alert. The point is that this A-B-C-D-E process will help you correct erroneous beliefs. You'll stop bashing yourself, and the catastrophic, self-loathing emotions will be replaced by feelings that are much more rational and appropriate for the unexpected event.

Some of what follows might feel repetitive, and it might sound as if you've heard it before. To a certain extent, you have, since I'm basically piecing out elements from the VAK model and earlier material about your drummer self-esteem.

Positive Self-Talk

As stated earlier, we listen to an almost constant internal flow of self-talk that involves questions or comments about ourselves or about people, places, and things in the world around us. So why not make the self-talk work *for* you rather than against you? The way to do that is to focus on what you want, rather than what you don't want. The language you use should focus on all the positives of getting up and performing for an audience.

Break out a few index cards and jot down the following ideas:

My drumming brings happiness and joy to my audience.
When I see someone moving to my music, this is an affirmation that I'm bringing something good into this world.
Because I've devoted many hours of practice to my art, I can allow myself to feel cool, calm, and collected when I perform before a crowd.

At first it may sound and feel a little contrived when you're programming positive self-talk, but it's better than having your mind run with internal statements like:

> I know I'm going to blow a fill during several songs tonight.
> I don't see anybody in the audience who looks happy, and there's no way we can win them over.
> I feel like I want to jump out of my skin.
> Why am I even doing this? I don't need this aggravation.

It's painful for me to even write such negative things that your mind can manufacture. Left unchecked, negative programming can sometimes become what mental health professionals call a self-fulfilling prophecy. To explain: Sometimes if you focus on an event with negative thoughts, your mind begins to practice all the things it needs to do in order to be successful at failing. You prophesize that it's going to happen, and the thoughts are fulfilled by your behavior.

I used to teach mental training skills to elite figure skaters. (Anxiety sometimes runs very high for them in both practice and in performance.) As an exercise, I'd have them write down three improvements in their skating that they wanted to make happen. Most of the time the young athletes reported that focusing on what they wanted to make happen was working. But one day a sad-faced skater came up to me, handed me a dog-eared index card, and said, "Your stuff doesn't work."

I replied, "Okay, let's figure out how it doesn't work."

I took a look at the card and knew the answer immediately. This is what she'd written:

> I won't get nervous.
> I won't fall on my axel.
> I won't travel on my spins.

Guess what was happening? She was getting extremely anxious on the ice, falling on each jump attempt and traveling (moving out of a circle) with every spin. Her mind didn't hear "won't." It heard and focused on "get nervous," "fall," and "travel." She was telling her mind what to do.

As an illustration, try to do the following:

Don't think about a big red balloon.

Don't think about a big yellow dog playing on a beach.

Don't think about your drumkit.

You can't *not* think of the pictures in the statements, can you? Your mind doesn't hear or pay attention to the words *don't* and *won't*. (Perhaps this is because it got very tired of hearing those words when you were a child.)

The solution for the young skater was simple and effective. We just changed her wording so she could focus her mind on what she wanted her body to do. These were her new statements:

I can stay calm and relaxed when I'm on the ice.

I can land my axel.

I can stay in the circle when I spin.

Here's another example of the power of directing and maintaining your focus. When I did some amateur bike racing, I always worried about crashing in the corners. I'd say to myself, "I don't want to crash in the corner." Consequently, I'd slow down, other cyclists would pass me, and I'd do poorly in the race. Totally frustrated, I approached the best bike racer in town, a guy named Andy. I asked him, "What do you think about when you're diving into a corner?"

In less than a second, he responded, "I think about keeping the bike upright." Andy focused on what he wanted and kept his mind off what he didn't want.

You can also decrease anxiety by running a mental success video in your mind. As you've done before, close your eyes and imagine yourself in a theater. You're the only member of the audience. See yourself on stage, relaxed and playing calmly. To further strengthen this image—and ideally the outcome—step into the movie and look out over your drums from the vantage point of sitting on your throne and playing in the emotional state that works best for you. Remember to bring in as many senses as possible—sight, sound, aroma, physical sensations (hands swinging the sticks, feet working the pedals, and so on), and internal feelings and emotions.

Anchoring is another technique that addresses performance anxiety. Here's one way to create an anchor for yourself. After a real "sizzle" (optimum/peak) practice where you feel you've played your best, take hold of the stick tips in some special way (perhaps just with the thumbs and forefingers) and recite—in your mind—the following statement: "If I can play it in practice, I can play it in performance." Just before a gig, grab hold of the stick tips in that same way, and the sensations of your optimum playing state should come flooding in.

Having a "letting go" ritual can also be very helpful for reducing anxiety. The easiest way to do this is to touch a doorframe—maybe coming into the club or out of the dressing room—and tell yourself, "I'm letting go of all harmful anxiety that may be harbored in my body, my mind, or both." Again, it's all trial and outcome. Try it, and see if this ritual works for you.

Reframing

I once volunteered to be a member of a pit crew at an amateur car race at Lime Rock Park in Connecticut. Moments before the race, I leaned in to wish the driver good luck. I saw all the elements of anxiety: His hands were shaking, his legs were twitching, he was stammering last-minute instructions to the pit crew boss, and he was licking his lips like his mouth was dry as a bone.

"You feeling anxious, Tony?" I asked.

"Hell, no!" he shot back. "I'm psyched!"

He had successfully reframed all the physical manifestations of anxiety into excitement.

Sometimes there's a thin line between anxiety and excitement, as high arousal of your nervous system is present in both states. You can sometimes ease anxiety into the land of excitement simply by renaming it. In doing so, you've reframed all the sensations you formerly labeled as anxiety into a state of being excited.

You can use the process of reframing for endless situations. Here are a few examples.

Original thought: "My drums are old."
Reframed thought: "My drums are vintage."

Original thought: "This club is small."
Reframed thought: "This club is quaint."

Original thought: "The audience is sparse."
Reframed thought: "The audience is intimate."

Original thought: "Our singer doesn't have much of a range."
Reframed thought: "Our singer has her own unique style."

You can also use a variation of reframing where you transform situations originally perceived as negative threats into occasions of positive challenge. Let's invent a couple.

Reframing Situation 1

You arrive at a gig and realize you've forgotten your hi-hat. There's no time to go home to retrieve it, and no family members or friends are available to bring it to you. You could have the following negative threat thought: "Man, what am I going to do? I've never played without a hi-hat. It's going to look wrong, and the songs are going to sound wrong!"

Or you could reframe the situation into a positive challenge thought: "Keith Moon often played without a hi-hat. If he can, I suppose I can too. I'll just throw what I normally play on the hi-hats to the ride cymbal, or maybe sometimes the bass drum hoop. It's not wrong, just different. There's room in drumming for a lot of experimenting with sounds and equipment, and tonight's my night to try something new."

Reframing Situation 2

Halfway into the second song of a gig you break your snare head, and you don't have a spare head or backup drum.

Negative threat thought: "There's no way I can finish the gig. The bandleader will have to end the set right now."

Positive challenge thought: "I'll just take one of my rack toms and place it in the snare stand. Luckily it has a coated head on it, so I can still play brushes. I'll tune it up tight, and it'll have to substitute for a snare. Come to think of it, a lot of the old R&B drummers placed their backbeats on toms."

Chemical

The chemical approach to dealing with stage fright utilizes anti-anxiety medications prescribed by a physician.

Don't kid yourself. The drummer who drinks a six-pack, shoots four ounces of tequila, or snorts a few lines of cocaine before he goes on stage is medicating himself for anxiety. I mention this because many individuals are averse to using pharmaceuticals to treat anxiety. You should keep an open mind about this subject. If greats such as Taylor Hawkins and Nigel Olsson can admit to experiencing anxiety, so can you. If this admission happens in the privacy of your personal physician's office, with the possibility of a prescription for medicine that will help, then so be it.

If you've tried all of the mechanical and cognitive methods for anxiety relief but it still has you in a stranglehold, you might want to consider discussing with your physician whether or not you'd be a good candidate for anti-anxiety medication. Just understand that your doctor might refer you to a psychiatrist first. This referral doesn't mean you have a major mental illness; it's simply the way some managed-care programs operate.

The two most common types of anti-anxiety medications are benzodiazepines and beta-blockers. Mention them by name should you speak with your doctor. He or she can give you all of the specific details on each one.

Fear

Fear is not the same as anxiety, although we tend to use them interchangeably in conversation. Fear is when three big, belligerent drunk guys with pointed cowboy boots threaten that if you don't play "Proud Mary" (for the fifth time that night), they're going to kick a hole in each of your drums. Fear is also when you're being chased down a dark alley by ninjas wielding swords and whipping Shuriken stars at you, or you look in your rearview mirror and see a stranger sitting in the back seat.

The difference between fear and anxiety is that in the fear scenario the threat is very real—it's right there in front of you. With anxiety, the stress is caused by the "what ifs" that live only in your mind.

Stress

People also confuse anxiety with stress. Stress (derived from *distress*) is caused by putting an organism—you—through too many changes in a limited period of time and not giving it time to adapt.

Let's use a guy named Gilbert to illustrate the state that we call stressed out. Gilbert is a widower with two grade-school-age kids. After getting his children ready for school, he's off to his day job as a service manager at a small car dealership. It's a forty-five-minute drive during rush hour. Along with having to sometimes deal with irate customers, Gilbert might also have to turn a wrench or two if one of his mechanics calls out sick. After work, Gilbert picks up his kids, feeds them dinner, and, if he can find a babysitter, often visits his elderly mom who lives in a nursing home.

Gilbert is also the drummer in a classic rock band that usually performs on Friday and Saturday nights. Lately Gilbert has been forgetting some of the beginnings, breaks, and endings of songs. He's often mentally frazzled and physically exhausted. The bandleader isn't happy with Gilbert's poor performances. Gilbert has been considering quitting the band because he's been feeling stressed out.

Does Gilbert *have* to quit his band? Of course not! But he will have to alter some behaviors because he's being put through too many changes and not having time to adapt. In this case, adaptation could consist of simply carving out a little alone time. To do so, Gilbert could hire someone or ask a relative to pick up his kids after school and make them dinner on Friday nights. That way he could relax at a coffee shop after work and mentally and physically get ready for the gig. Or he could schedule a massage to ease the muscles that are knotted due to the excessive emotional stress (crabby customers, dealing with his aging mother) and physical stress (mechanical work) in his life.

Some heavier changes that Gilbert could enact would include finding a job at a larger car dealership that's closer to home. That way he wouldn't be saddled with extra work, and the shorter commute would help reduce the daily stress of having to deal with rush-hour traffic. He could also hire someone to pick up his kids and make dinner for his family on a daily basis. This would cause Gilbert to make accommodations for the extra expense, but the rewards of feeling less stress—on and off the stage—could be worth it.

Stress can be just as damaging to your drumming career as long-term, unchecked performance anxiety. Before you hit the point of burnout in some or all areas of your life, do what you can to make behavioral changes that will lessen your stress factor.

Mistakes

If what's driving your performance anxiety is the thought that you'll be evaluated negatively, then you're most likely obsessing about not wanting to make a mistake. But mistakes happen. Consider the expression "If you stumble, make it part of the dance."

I know of a top-notch drummer whose technique is such that he holds his sticks as loosely as possible. He believes this provides him with his optimum playing form. On a regular basis, however, he'll lose his grip, and a stick will go flying out of his hand. At first glance it looks as if he's made a mistake. But without missing a beat, this drummer will deliberately toss the other stick into the air or out into the audience, making it appear as though the first one also flew out of his hand on purpose. He stumbled, but he made it part of the dance.

Figure skaters make a lot of mistakes. The major one is falling, usually when trying to land a jump. When I worked with elite figure skaters, I was always emphasizing that what matters is how you handle it when you fall. I told skaters that after a fall they needed to get back on their feet as soon as possible. Some became so expert at getting vertical again that it looked like they literally bounced up off the ice!

Why was this so important? When a skater falls, the crowd gasps and then groans. This calls attention to the mistake and, consciously or unconsciously, could influence the judges. By lying on the ice, the fallen skater only highlights the mistake. The faster the skater gets up, the better the chance that everyone concerned, including the judges, will move past the fall and on to the next jump or spin.

When you make a drumming mistake in performance, calling attention to it—grimacing, cursing, throwing a stick, or shaking your head in disgust—highlights the mistake and makes its effect more lasting and damaging. It's like shining a megawatt spotlight on yourself and calling out, "Hey, everybody, I just screwed up!" From a psychological perspective, calling unnecessary attention to a mistake can wreak havoc on your drummer self-esteem.

On the flip side, I've also seen drummers smile, laugh, make a goofy face, or show no expression at all when they've done something that some people would consider a mistake. The choice of reaction is yours. You can either call some very major and negative attention to your bungle, or you can lighten the experience and move on. Or you can make like it never happened, because, after all, the audience might not have caught your error in the first place.

Now for a story…

In Tibet, Buddhist monk novitiates aspire to enter into the "room of enlightenment." Before they can do this, however, they must pass through the "hall of 1,000 terrors." These terrors contain all the novitiates' worst anxieties and self-doubts, and they appear in both image and sound.

Once the novitiates enter the hall of terrors, the door locks behind them and there is no turning back. The only way out is through the hall and into the room of enlightenment.

While waiting for their turn to enter the hall, the anxious and apprehensive novitiates turn to the wise old monks for advice and wisdom. With a knowing smile, the older monks whisper the following words into their ears: "Just keep your feet moving."

Chapter 7: Band Dynamics

> *"When you're living in a world that you don't understand, find a few good buddies, start a band."*
>
> —from "Start A Band," recorded by
> Brad Paisley and Keith Urban

When you first start a band, or when you're selected to join an existing band after an audition process, everything is all rosy, shiny, and new—for you, anyway. You may have great aspirations and expectations for where you and your group are going. You're happy, upbeat, and excited.

Welcome to the honeymoon period. Part of the reason why this stage is so enjoyable is that you're usually deeply immersed in the creative process. Whether you're learning a working band's repertoire or building set lists with a start-up group, you're drumming!

But here's the rub. The creative act of making music often blinds you to many of the mundane aspects of being a band member. Although you're having a ball playing music with your new compadres, it's important to ask some critical questions during this crucial beginning stage. By doing so, you'll save yourself some major headaches once you move out of the honeymoon period and into more of the business side of playing in a band.

Here are just a few things you might want to inquire about.

Is there a bandleader? What are the leader's responsibilities? Does he or she get a bigger cut of the take-home pay?

Who selects the songs? If you have a bandleader, is it a strict autocracy, or are songs chosen through a more democratic process?

Who does the booking? Has one member been designated, or does everyone make attempts at finding gigs? If someone has been designated (or has volunteered), does that person get a higher percentage of the pay?

Does the band want or have a manager or agent? If so, what are his or her duties?

And, most important, what is the common goal for how far everyone in the band wants to take the project? Does the band want to tour? Is it trying to become an opening act for a national touring group? Is the band looking for a major record deal? Is there the possibility that the members will want to move to a major city with the idea of increasing the chances of being discovered by a talent scout? Or is everyone content with remaining a working club band in the local area? If that's the case, how many gigs does the band want to play per month?

It's important to ask these questions when all members are present. Even with an established working band, you might be surprised to find that these issues have never been discussed.

To avoid all of the business aspects of a band—and sometimes the hassles involved with getting paid for your services—you can join or start a group that gets together to simply have fun. You may spend Sunday afternoons in a very loose, relaxed session where you play what-ever songs you want. Add some beverages and snacks and you have a low-key, enjoyable weekend activity with no worries about booking gigs or having to deal with club owners who don't want to fork over their cash at the end of the night.

You could also simply duck into your practice space whenever you get a chance and play solo. You can jam along to CDs or just bash away for a while in your own freeform style.

If you *do* decide to join a group that has aspirations of taking things to the next level, be aware that many bands fail to make it out of the begin-ning stage. Why? Most often, while these bands were honing their live show to near perfection, they never paid attention to the business end of a career in music. Compound this with individuals who are skittish, shy, or afraid to ask club owners for a gig, and the group could soon disinte-grate due to a lack of professional progress. If you want to increase the odds that your band will stay together, ask the questions listed above.

The Middle Stage

If a band has been together for a while (a few months to a few years, depending on the rate of progression), we can say it's in its middle stages. Let's imagine a mythical band that's doing well. There's a comfort level among the members, they have a devoted following, and everyone's on the same page regarding such matters as repertoire, rehearsals, and number of gigs per month.

In many ways, a band in this stage is like a family. Everyone is tolerant of each other's quirks, idiosyncrasies, strengths, and weaknesses. Things are stable, and nobody has quit or stalked off stage in a hissy fit. You could say that the Rolling Stones have been in a seemingly endless middle stage. With the exception of a few members coming and going, they're still a strong unit, even after several decades.

But what if, after the tingle of the honeymoon period wears off, things aren't so pleasant? What you initially thought was an amusing behavior by a bandmate is now a major annoyance. Yes, you have gigs and a following, but the music has grown stale and soggy. And you are starting to feel that your performances are lackluster. Your website needs a redesign, your Facebook page hasn't been updated in months, and your street team has disbanded due to lack of interest. Members wander into practice late and/or indifferent. Rehearsals are canceled without explanation or simply forgotten. Being a member of this band is quickly becoming a chore.

What do you do? First ask yourself if you want to try to salvage the band before it dissolves into oblivion. If so, you'll need to take a proactive stance and start making bold and honest statements about the deterioration of the group. Above all, you need to communicate that this band means a lot to you and that you're willing to fight for its continuance. If you have a designated bandleader, take your concerns to that person first. Ask whether he or she wants to address the issues or if you should speak to the rest of the group directly. Remember that your goal is to remedy the situation, or at least get the band on the road to recovery. If you're the one who talks to your bandmates, remember to make "I" statements, avoid name calling and accusations, and outline what you'd like to see changed. (Refer back to Chapter 5 for other tools and strategies.) The difference here is that you're not confronting one single person; you're addressing the entire group in your pitch to revive the band.

When you decide to air your concerns, let your passion for the band show. Just make sure the setting is positive and intimate. You may want to call a group meeting at a local coffeehouse, diner, or someplace other than where you rehearse. Your statements might sound something like:

"I'm really afraid that our band is slowly coming apart. I don't want that to happen. I want the band to survive."

"I have so much invested in this band, but lately my motivation to play feels like it's slipping away, and I feel like you can hear it in my drumming. It's becoming mechanical."

"I don't think I have all the answers to fix this situation, but I was wondering if changing up the music could provide the boost we need."

As you air your concerns, be sure to field questions, and do your best to avoid getting angry if someone mocks or attacks you. If at least one other member proposes some type of strategy that would breathe new life into your band, the others may follow.

The Big Ending

"You're fired!" Have you ever heard those words from a bandleader? I've been fired a total of four times over my forty-five-year career as a drummer and percussionist. The aspect I find most interesting about these "involuntary separations" is that none of them were directly related to my drumming skills.

I mentioned earlier that a band can be like a family. Unfortunately, families can be quite dysfunctional. In the honeymoon phase of a band, most members show a strong public persona, but as the group moves into the middle stages, the members begin to reveal their full range of personality traits. Sometimes many of those traits aren't so pretty, and sometimes they're quite disturbing. But how were you to know that when you first auditioned or formed your band? You couldn't have. Only the passage of time would allow these negative aspects of self to come through.

Unless it's for something obvious, like substance abuse, you may never know the real reason why you were let go. Don't waste time trying to figure it out. There are millions of reasons for being cut loose, and many times those reasons are completely irrational. Regardless of the reason, if it's not handled properly on a mental and emotional level, being fired can put a huge dent in your drummer self-esteem or even put you in a state of depression that could interfere with your day-to-day life.

The ending of your involvement with a band can be considered a form of death. Elisabeth Kübler-Ross gave us five stages in the death and dying process:

1. Denial
2. Bargaining
3. Depression/sadness
4. Anger
5. Acceptance

Denial is when you hear the words come out of the bandleader's (or manager/agent's) mouth, and you just can't believe it. You may ask why and get some vague, obscure answer, like, "It just wasn't working out," or, "We're looking for a different sound," or, "You just don't seem to fit with the rest of the band." You might press for specifics, but, again, don't expect a clear, concise answer to be forthcoming.

Bargaining is when you try to haggle your way back into the band. You seize upon the slightest notion of why you might have been fired, and you promise to fix it. You may say, "If you're looking for a different sound, I could try an electronic kit or add some hand percussion," or, "I could grow my hair longer, dye it purple, and get a few tattoos," or, "I'd be willing to take a cut in pay if you keep me on." You might be able to wheedle your way back in, but usually when the decision has been made that you're out, it sticks.

Depression/sadness is when the reality of the situation is starting to sink in. You're out and not getting back in. Attempts at bargaining have fallen on deaf ears. For some drummers, this depression/sadness becomes pervasive and all encompassing. You might spend your days remembering how fantastic the band was (although you're prone to some revisionist history when you're depressed) and mentally reliving your glory days. Worse, though, you could isolate yourself from the world, develop problems with eating and sleeping, and let this one experience allow you to question the value of life itself.

Anger often appears when you determine a target. Drunk-dialing the bandleader, manager, agent, or whoever had the task of telling you to hit the bricks wouldn't be uncommon during this stage. Like depression, anger can become all consuming and destructive if it lasts too long or intensifies over time.

Special note: If, during the depression and anger stages of grief, you should begin to have thoughts of hurting yourself or others, please seek out the services of a qualified mental-health provider. There will always be another band for you, and—once you're thinking clearly again—you will realize that a loss such as this never warrants harming yourself or another person.

Acceptance doesn't mean that you begin shouting to the world, "Yippee, I got fired!" It's more a quiet acknowledgement that unfair, unpleasant, and irrational events happen to all of us. You begin to move on with your life. You take tangible steps toward joining or starting a different band.

Someday I'd like to talk with Mick Jagger of the Rolling Stones and ask him how he's held his band together for so many years. A fellow musician recently asked me how many bands I'd been in over the span of my career. I stopped counting after twenty-five.

Maybe the point is to enjoy your current band, knowing that nothing lasts forever. All things pass, and the only constant in life is change. Or, as a wise old philosopher once told me, "Life is a series of hellos and good-byes."

Chapter 8: Mind Matters

The questions and answers in this chapter are reprints from my bi-monthly advice column in *Modern Drummer*, which was developed to offer creative advice, strategies, and solutions for mental issues that are common among aspiring musicians. They're not meant to solve severe psychological and/or psychiatric problems that would be better addressed through counseling with a qualified mental health practitioner.

A+ Practice, C- Performance (May 2009)

In the past year I got a chance to play with two different "name" performers. The rehearsals went well, and I thought I was prepared. But during the actual performances I felt my drumming was barely adequate. Moments before going on stage, I was psyched and I didn't have stage fright, but I just couldn't turn it on. The artists seemed satisfied with my playing—no negative comments—but I walked away believing I'd turned in a C-minus performance. I'm trying to figure out what happened. Can you help?

Sure. You're just not good enough. Does that nail it? If you had an instant visceral reaction to that statement—like a punch in the gut—then my guess is probably spot on.

See, there's a part of you that had the self-confidence to accept the gig; you believed in your abilities enough to say yes. You also sailed through the rehearsals with these known musicians using that same part of your brain. But when it came time to play the gig, another part of you was operating. We'll call that self-doubt.

First, as I always recommend, try to recall any inner dialogue that you were aware of just before the gig. You mentioned that you were psyched, so that inner-speak was probably quite positive and powerful. But were snippets of any other words or phrases in your mind expressing self-doubt?

If you're in your late teens to late twenties, this self-doubt is a result of what some psychologists have termed "the imposter syndrome." You think you've got the world fooled into believing you're a good drummer. You may have spent 10,000 hours woodshedding (which is known to be the minimal amount of practice time required to "master" a particular skill), but some part of you still insists on believing that it's not enough and that you're a fraud, eventually to be found out.

If you got the call to play with two well-known artists, I'm guessing you have a pretty good reputation and will have other opportunities to dazzle your audience while backing up a "name" performer. You've obviously prepared yourself physically—through practice and rehearsal—so start to incorporate some techniques that will prepare you mentally. Try these:

1. Close your eyes. Picture a screen. On that screen, place memories of all your "sizzling" drum performances—times when you played great. Make the images big, bright, and in colors that really pop. Imagine stepping into at least one of those experiences, and relive the glory. See what you saw, hear what you heard, and feel what you felt at the time.

2. On a 3x5 index card, write the following sentence: "If I can do it in practice, I can do it in performance." Keep the card with you until these words are committed to memory.

3. Check your physiology as you walk on stage at your next gig. Keep your shoulders back and your head held high, and wear a smile—not a phony one. If you get in touch with your love of drums and drumming and you appreciate your hard-earned chops, that smile should come naturally.

4. If you end up tuning in to a scared inner voice that doubts your ability, reassure it with a confident, knowing voice. If the scared voice persists, refute it with facts—facts based on real-life experiences that prove you're a good player.

Regarding your C-minus gigs, give yourself credit for getting the job done. Granted, you didn't strut your best stuff like you had hoped. But it wasn't a disaster either. You probably just played it safe.

Dumps And Dives: Getting Through The Night (July 2009)

When I load my gear into a club, my first few reactions influence the way I play over the course of the night. Specifically, if the club is a bit trashy, with very few people milling about, my motivation takes a nosedive and my playing suffers. Any way I can change this?

Absolutely! You can't change the appearance of the club or the fact that the place is sparsely populated, but you can change what you're telling yourself about the situation. First off, tune in to your inner dialogue, the voice in your head that's commenting on the first few images your eyes notice. What is it telling you? What's the tone? Most likely, it's a negative voice in a depressing tone that may be—erroneously—blaming *you* for the crummy appearance of the club.

For example: "What a dump. If the band was better, we'd be getting better gigs. Or if *I* was better, we'd be getting better gigs. The band sucks; I suck."

That type of negative inner chatter can make you feel miserable. And when you feel that way, your playing is obviously going to suffer. Your mindset has become totally toxic!

The reality is that you have no evidence to support any of those notions, other than the fact that the club could use a good cleaning. But it is what it is, and you got the gig. So start to refute some of your negative statements, making sure that your internal voice remains upbeat and positive.

For example, tell yourself something like this: "It's Saturday night, and I've got a paying gig. I'll bet there are a lot of drummers sitting at home *wishing* they were playing. I'm not here to evaluate the decor of this club. I'm here to play my drums and indulge my passion. Even if the only customers in this place decide to split after one song, I can always look at tonight as a 'paid practice.' And I can use the money I've earned to buy that cymbal stand I need."

What you want to do is shift your state of mind from one of negativity—which will most likely influence your performance in a detrimental way—to one of "an attitude of gratitude." Your outlook needs to be in the realm of, "I'm here. I'm ready to play, and I *want* to play."

After you've set up your drums, introduce yourself to someone at the bar who appears friendly. Thank that person for coming out. Now you've made a personal contact and set up the possibility that a fan might come see you at another gig. These momentary encounters can help build your fan base to the point where you're eventually playing to larger audiences in much nicer venues. But at the very least, you should feel satisfied if your music reaches just *one* person at this particular gig.

Realize that when you're performing, you're sharing the gift of music. Perhaps you're helping audience members let go of a bad day or feel inspired to work through a rough spot in their life. Music is powerful, and music is healing. So play on—with joy—no matter where you are.

Releasing The Pressure Of Sitting In (September 2009)

Many years ago, when I was in my twenties, I was fortunate to play with a band that had a couple of regional hit singles. Now when I'm at a party or a wedding where there's a band playing, someone always *asks me to sit in. The bandleader inevitably introduces me as some sort of "rock star," even though it's been years since I've felt anything close to that. I take a seat behind the kit, and feelings of dread and an almost paralyzing anxiety set in. I think* everyone *is watching my every move and expecting me to play something flashy. When the song ends, even though I receive applause, I feel I didn't meet expectations. Any advice?*

You're under no obligation to sit in, so why put yourself through the agony? You can always say you're not in the mood to play. But I'm guessing you'd ultimately like to be able to sit in and truly *enjoy* the experience. Two things are ruining that possibility: fear of negative evaluation, and erroneous thinking.

Let's pretend you agree to sit in and you struggle from the first bar. You're rushing and dragging, blowing fills...

So what happens then? Are you sent to Siberia for ten years of hard labor? Of course not. I'm sure you beat yourself up for a while afterward, but nothing *really* bad happens. And here's the real kicker: Some, or maybe even most, of the audience never even noticed your mistakes or your anxiety. But because your erroneous thinking had you believing that all eyes were glued to you, you manufactured a huge fear of being evaluated negatively.

Although someone's eyes may be looking at you, don't assume that he or she is *thinking* about you. More likely, the people at the party are worrying whether the kids are okay at home with the new babysitter, or they're plotting a dance with a bridesmaid.

Of course, a few musicians at the party probably watched intently as you flubbed your way through the song. But so what? It's over, and you'll get another shot at playing again. Everyone can have a bad day once in a while. Just learn from it and move on. Next time, try to focus on how much *fun* it is to be able to play music and entertain your friends, even if you don't have the same panache you once had.

Getting Unstuck From Drummer's Block (December 2009)
I've been playing with an alt-rock band for about seven years. We perform primarily originals, so my job is to establish my own grooves and fills, as opposed to copying whatever's been played on a cover song. As of late, however, I feel I'm running out of ideas, and finding the right beat is becoming more and more difficult. It's stressing me out. Can you help?

First, take a deep breath and relax. The anxiety you've created surrounding this situation is blocking your concentration. Remember back in school when the more nervous you became about an upcoming test, the worse you did on the exam? It's the same thing here—anxiety blocks concentration.

The best way to predict the future is to look to the past. Have you been able to create grooves and fills preceding this current block? Of course you have. So you have every reason to believe you can keep doing your job. You may be thinking too hard. And you may be thinking irrationally, in the sense that, in your words, you're "running out of ideas." That's absurd! The musical vocabulary is unlimited; you're the one holding yourself back. Try easy. Think about those two words and really let them sink in. *Try easy.*

Writer Clarissa Pinkola Estés recommends that when you're blocked, you should get away from your chosen field—in this case rock music and drumming—and just observe others creating art in their chosen discipline. Visit a museum, listen to a string quartet, watch a street performer, or catch a magic show. These activities inspire creativity in new and fresh ways that you can later apply to your drumming.

World-class drummer/percussionist Walfredo Reyes Jr. once told me, "To find fresh new sounds, dig deep into the roots." He's absolutely right. But I know from dispensing this information in the past that many drummers discard his wisdom because they're wedded to the sound of the rock music that's out there now. Get some old CDs, and listen to the way drummers played rock 'n' roll in the 1950s and '60s. For instance, they might've played a ride pattern on their bass drum hoop rather than on the bell of a cymbal. Different, right? Take it a step further. Locate some old recordings from when drummers first started piecing together sets, which were often referred to as "trap kits." Listen to the way they incorporated woodblocks, triangles, and other "traps" (short for *contraptions*) into the songs.

Physically break up, or mix up, your drum setup, either during your own woodshedding or when practicing with your band. We all gravitate to familiar patterns and comfort zones, and the way we have our drums and cymbals arranged is no different. Scale down to just hi-hat and snare. Gradually add drums and cymbals, maybe at slightly different or even radical angles. Then accept the challenge of trying to play in this fashion. The change in your setup just might result in shaking loose some new ideas stuck somewhere in the creative recesses of your brain.

One last point: Declare yourself a drummer. Words can be extremely powerful, and how we hear them spoken in our own voice can have a tremendous impact on our self-concept about what we have the ability—or inability—to create. Out loud, speak the words "I'm a drummer." Notice how that feels. Strong. Confident.

Now speak the phrase "I play drums." Or, worse yet, "I play the drums." (Notice how "the" has a distancing quality.) These last two ways of describing your relationship with your instrument tend to have a weakening effect on your perception of your abilities.

It's time for you to bounce—your band needs its drummer.

The Perfectionist (January 2010)
After working with a talented singer/songwriter/producer for several years now, I've defined a pattern in my dealings with him. We'll lay down a couple takes, get a positive vibe going, and after the third or fourth take I feel as though I've

produced at least one or two solid drum tracks. But here's where the problem begins. He wants to keep going, all the while giving me very specific and minute criticisms, plus suggestions. After the eighth or ninth take, I'm confused, frustrated, angry, and more than a little insecure about my drumming. Is there a way I can keep the vibe flowing while still addressing this artist's suggestions?

I hope you're charging a decent studio rate for this headache. In all likelihood, it isn't your drumming that's not meeting his specs, but his perception of the entire composition and/or his playing. But because you're the hired gun—the employee—it's easier to blame *you* for what his ears don't like. Starting to question his own abilities might be much too frightening for him. You're an easy target; he can deflect his true feelings of inadequacy on you. Of course, understanding this probably helps you feel only a *little* better about the situation. Besides, insight alone isn't usually a strong agent of change.

So let's move into an action plan that could remedy your situation. I want to illuminate two choices for you.

Plan A: Negotiate. Take this artist out for coffee or lunch before your next scheduled session. Getting him out of the studio levels the playing field. In the studio, you work for him in an employer/employee relationship. Changing the physical context helps to alter or disrupt the power structure. At a diner or restaurant, it's just two musicians discussing a project.

After a bit of chitchat, ease your way into why you wanted to meet with him. Begin a conversation about how in the '70s Steely Dan hired a host of A-list drummers for their albums and had each drummer play his interpretation of the same songs. Leaders Walter Becker and Donald Fagen then chose what sounded best to their ears, and those takes made it onto the records. Obviously, with such drumming royalty in the studio, you continue to tell him, the choice was not made on technical prowess but rather was based on style, feel, and other often indefinable traits.

Now zero in. Inform your perfectionist producer that you've found from your experience that your best drumming—the type that defines your style and feel—is usually created in the range of one to four takes. After that, you find yourself over-thinking a piece, concentrating too hard, experiencing creative fatigue—however you want to phrase it. In this way, you're not blaming him for anything. There's no reason for him to defend himself. You're simply explaining how you work. Ask him to agree that, barring flubs and clams, the two of you will hold your tracking sessions to no more than four takes the next time you're in the studio. During that time, he's more than welcome to make suggestions and add to the creative process. (Remind him, though, that he's forking over cash for your expertise. You're the drummer.)

If he agrees to your new arrangement, in the future you'll avoid his prolonged neurotic babbling of criticisms and tips in your ear. As such, you won't be in danger of being pushed to the point where you're calling him an anal-retentive nitpicker. The main thing is that you've established a new pattern, one that preserves your sanity and self-esteem and is likely to result in your best drumming.

Plan B: Bow out gracefully. What if he refuses? Let's imagine this producer dismisses your pitch and insists you keep cutting takes "until it's right," thereby retaining the old pattern that's driving you bonkers.

You have the right to bow out of the arrangement; no one is forcing you to stay. This guy is renting a lot of space in your head. And unless he's paying you boatloads of cash, is all the aggravation worth it?

First, suggest that you may not be the right drummer for his music. (You've already laid the foundation for this statement by speaking of the multitude of Steely Dan drummers and the bandleaders' eventually finding the style and feel they decided matched with their songs.)

Perhaps he doesn't buy it. You're his drummer, he wants only you, and he's unwilling to relinquish his existing system of creating songs. You take it a step further. Here's where what your mom and dad taught you comes into play: Honesty is the best policy. You tell him it's just not working for you anymore. If he wants reasons, tell him the truth. The hovering, the flow of criticisms, the "over-baked takes." Be prepared for an emotional reaction from him, but remember that you're in a business relationship and you're choosing to end it. As a professional, you should come prepared with the names of some other studio players to recommend, even though he may not accept them. Wish him the best of luck in his career, say goodbye, and move on to your next client.

Concentration Problems (March 2010)

I've been playing drums for about four months now, and I'm having serious problems concentrating on learning and practicing. I've been trying to count out loud, as all of my instruction books suggest, but when I do, I lose focus and start messing up. My hands don't follow my count, and I start playing the wrong thing altogether. Then I get mad and give up. Do you have any suggestions on how to strengthen my focus? I find that concentration problems show up in other areas of my life as well.

First off, take a deep breath in. Hold it, and then exhale fully. Relax. You're trying way too hard with this whole thing, and it's making you uptight—uptight in your mind *and* your body. Try easy. Perform this simple little relaxation exercise *before* you begin each of your practice sessions.

Now let's continue with an important question. Is there anything else that's drawing your attention in a powerful way when you sit down at your drums? Something that's a consistent theme or problem? A girlfriend? A boyfriend? A conflict with another student, a coworker, or a family member? If that's the case, you'll probably need to deal with that first. Find some resolution before you can clear your mind for a good session with your drums.

Motivation is a huge factor in any learning process. What attracted you to the drums in the first place? Their look? Their sound? Now for the hard question: Does the *reality* of playing drums come close to the *fantasy* that you originally had in your mind? I used to think/fantasize about playing guitar. Once I bought a guitar and started to learn to play, I quickly lost motivation. The reality of actually playing did not match the fantasy I'd held before I bought the instrument. I hated fretting the strings and contorting my fingers to make a sound. I later admitted to myself that I was in love with the shape and color of my guitar. If I hadn't sold it, it probably would have wound up on the wall, not unlike a poster or a painting. Something nice to look at, but that's about all.

Putting aside the concentration issue for a moment, do you feel motivated—even though you're struggling right now—to play your drums? If the answer is yes, keep at it! If the answer is no, you might want to experiment with another instrument. If you think you'd like to stay in the percussion family, try a hand drum like a djembe or a conga.

Words are very powerful and carry connotations that can influence our moods and actions. Let's look at the word *practice*. When you were very young, you practiced how to eat with a fork and a spoon. Later, you practiced multiplication and division. And you practiced how to throw a football or baseball. But over time the word *practice* can start to become associated with drudgery and work. You begin to see it as a chore rather than as an opportunity to better your skills or just have some fun. So, begin thinking of your time with drumming as *playing* your drums, rather than going in to *practice* them. Tell yourself, and whoever else is in the room (friends, family, etc.), that you're going in to *play* on your practice pad, snare drum, or full kit.

You mention instructional books, and I just mentioned a practice pad. Learning how to read drum music and having the convenience of playing with sticks on a pad are both important, but make sure you're spending time with real drums and just cutting loose on the kit. If you don't have a drumset and cymbals yet, see about renting some gear or buying a used entry-level kit through your local music store or Craigslist. Alternate your time with the instructional books with playing along to your favorite CDs or MP3s. Allow yourself to enjoy the feel of the smooth sticks in your hands, the sound of the drums and cymbals, the sensation of your foot coming down on the pedal, the beater striking the kick drum head…. Have fun with your drums.

You can build concentration skills in many ways. Buy jigsaw puzzles, and work with them *only* up until they stop being fun and challenging. When you start to feel frustrated, walk away and come back to them later. Or try crosswords or sudokus. Watch episodes of game shows, and answer the questions. Again, perform these activities only until you start to feel frustrated and it stops being fun. Walk away and do something different, but make sure to return to the activity later.

Acquiring any new skill takes time and is a challenge. You mention you've been playing for only four months. Cut yourself some slack! The pros you see live in concert make it look easy, but they've put in *thousands* of hours behind the kit.

You also mention that you get mad and give up. Anger is an emotion that in this case isn't helping you build a drumming skill set. When you start to feel anger or frustration rising within you, stop what you're doing and try something different. If you're already at your drums, play free-form for a while until the anger passes.

I'd be remiss if I didn't mention one last possibility for your problem. I'm sure you've heard of ADD—attention deficit disorder. You say this concentration issue shows up in other parts of your life. If all of my suggestions fail you, it might be worth your time to be evaluated by a qualified health provider—a physician, a psychologist, a social worker—who specializes in ADD. If you're diagnosed with attention deficit disorder, a physician will most likely prescribe a medication that will help you focus.

If your motivation is true and you've cleared out any powerful problems or distractions that are pulling your attention away from your drums, and if you've ruled out ADD, I say stick with it, try easy, and *play*, and your skills *will* come.

Removing Inner And Outer Obstacles (May 2010)

After attending music school in my country, Slovakia, where I took lessons for guitar and drums, I realized the only thing I want to play is the drums. I try to play as much as I can every day, watch music videos focused on drumming, read magazines, and do whatever I can that's linked to drumming. I think about it a lot, but sometimes I feel sad that I'm not improving. I know that playing drums for just one year isn't going to make my skills great—it's something you need to do for your entire life to be good. But sometimes I think I don't have a chance to be good because I'm a girl. Some men drummers are not so friendly to me. Plus my parents don't understand why I want to play drums, and that's why I do not have my own drumkit. Please help.

Thanks for writing. I'm very glad that you're so passionate about being a drummer. Passion and motivation go hand in hand and will help you overcome the obstacles that you'll inevitably meet as you make your way along your drumming path.

Let's talk about beliefs and expectations. You worry about not improving, but in the next sentence you admit—and realize—that if you've been playing for only one year you can't expect your skills to be great. You may have hit a bit of a plateau where your playing seems like it's not moving forward, but that will pass. And here's the kicker: You're better today than you were a year ago, right? Be glad, and own that accomplishment! You stuck with it, and you are, at your current level, contributing your own unique drum voice to the world. Be proud! Skill acquisition for an instrument comes at varying rates for each player. (It took me two years to master a solid conga slap.) So keep up your daily practice, and, as you say, do everything you can that's linked to drumming. That which we think about, we do. That which we do, we become. You're engaged in all the right activities—physical practice, watching videos, reading magazines—that will continue to build your drumming skill set.

Speaking of practice, we live in a fast-paced world and often try to multitask—sometimes working on too many different things in a single block of time. Make sure that when you rehearse you focus on your drums only, cutting out any distractions that may be in your environment. Turn off your cell phone and the TV, and alert your friends and family that you need this block of time to keep developing your drumming.

The men drummers who are "not so friendly" to you are a bunch of jerks. There are a couple of reasons why they may be acting this way toward you. They may be misogynists (men who hate women). Or they don't think women belong behind a drumkit and believe you should be playing a more "ladylike" instrument, such as flute or violin. Unfortunately, many individuals in our society have preconceived notions about what professions or activities should fall into the category of male or female. Again, these men you speak of may harbor a belief that women shouldn't be drummers. Of course, women can engage in any profession or hobby they desire, which leads me to my next guess: These men are threatened by you. Perhaps you are a more proficient player than they are, or they fear that someday you will be.

Don't let people intimidate you or diminish your love of drums and drumming. Realize that inadequate individuals like this will always exist in the world, but stay strong in your passions and pursuits. (Maybe you can have a T-shirt made that says "Female Drummers Rule!") Also, surf the Web and see if you can find any female drummer support groups—or start one yourself.

Finally, let's discuss your parents. Have you ever asked them why they seem averse to your drumming and won't allow you to have your own drumset? I have a couple hunches as to why, but regardless, you need to have a real heart-to-heart conversation with them where you express your love and passion for the art of drumming.

Here's one hunch. Although they paid for your lessons and came to your gigs, perhaps they fear that you want to make drumming your full-time profession. Their expectation for you may be different, more along the lines of having a conventional nine-to-five job or becoming a doctor, lawyer, etc. Ask them.

Unfortunately, rock music and rock musicians are often associated with a decadent lifestyle marked by heaving drinking and drug use. Ask your parents if they fear you'll get caught up in this, and then assure them that you won't. I think the solution lies in opening more lines of communication. Keep asking questions and making requests, always with a cool head, not allowing your anger or frustration to be present in the discussions.

In closing, celebrate your unique contributions to the world of music, and always remember that you have the right to pursue your passion for drumming. Rock on!

Competitions And Auditions (August 2010)

A few years ago, when I was in high school, my group was in a battle of the bands. We didn't win—we weren't even in the top three. The guys in the band blamed me because I was nervous and sped up the tempos too much. I later quit the group because I felt guilty about messing things up for them. This past year I entered a drum competition at a local music store and was cut after the first round. Then I auditioned for a band and didn't get the job. I'm not playing with anyone right now, and I'm thinking of learning to play guitar instead. But I think what I want is to play drums in a band again. I'm really kind of confused.

I've got a question for you: What's another name for the second-place finisher in a competition? Answer: loser.

Do I really mean that? Of course not. I simply wanted to get your attention fast and shoot straight to the heart of your problem. Because of your interpretation of the events you mention and their unwanted outcomes, I'll bet you've judged and labeled yourself a loser. There's a very thick thread that runs through your letter, and it can be summarized as "better than/less than" or "winner/loser."

Let's start with your debacle at the battle of the bands. You'll need to let go of that experience in order to move on and make a clear-headed decision on whether to stick with drumming or try expressing yourself through another instrument. Try this: Close your eyes and imagine one of those old 12" black-and-white televisions. Turn it on. Now, on the TV screen see yourself performing in that band competition and hear the music. Watch yourself speeding up the song tempos. (If you're feeling twinges of discomfort or pain, you're performing this exercise correctly. Stick with it; hang in.) Maybe you see the other guys giving you nasty looks or you notice your face frozen in fear. After a couple minutes, start to make the image fuzzy, like when your cable TV is acting up. At the same time, begin to turn down the music. Notice whether your discomfort begins to lessen. Now fade the image to black and turn off the TV. Gone. All that's left is a blank screen. No images, no music.

Remind yourself that your drumming has improved since your high school years. How can I make this assumption? Since you had these experiences a few years ago, you've likely put in some practice time that strengthened your chops. I don't know if you're still speeding up tempos, but maybe you've overcome that tendency. If you, as you are now, were able to go back in time, that experience may never have happened. But you have to accept and celebrate the drummer you are *today*. By revivifying your memory of the battle of the bands, you're only keeping yourself stuck in the past. The previous exercise should have helped fade the memory. But should that recollection pop into your awareness again, don't fight it. Eventually it will get tired of terrorizing you, and your attention will soon be snagged by something else.

If you're still rushing your grooves in front of an audience, it's probably due to stage fright/performance anxiety. Find a method that puts you in the zone for playing. Relaxation CDs, yoga, and physical exercise are just a few of the things that can help you calm yourself before a gig. See which ones work for you.

Finally, and perhaps most important, begin to move away from thinking of drumming as a competitive sport. If you want competition, play a video game or join a hockey league. Begin to think more in terms of what you can add to the universe of music. If you want to compete in the field of music, compete against yourself. Challenge yourself to be the best drummer you can be.

We live in a highly competitive society, so it's only natural that competitions would leak into the world of music. There were highly publicized "drum battles" between big-name drummers back in the 1940s and '50s. But was it really a competition? I don't think so. It was more of a way to showcase the superb skills of drummers of that era to a totally enamored audience. But somewhere along the line, things got much more serious. Look at the popularity of *American Idol*, with winners becoming superstars almost overnight. In the drum competition world, the winner takes home prize money and high-end gear. And the rest of the competitors—like you—often walk away feeling like losers.

Obviously there's a place for competition in drumming. Drum corps hold competitions every summer. But the rules of engagement and what the judges are seeking in those situations are clearly defined. I'm not so sure that's the case with battles of the bands and contests sponsored by music stores. Prefer-ences in drumming and tastes in music are extremely subjective. Keep in mind that some drummers are highly competitive adrenaline junkies that crave any opportunity for a thrill. That's cool. Different strokes for different folks. It'd be a very dull world if we were all identical. But from your letter, that doesn't sound like you. And remember, you chose to put yourself in those three competitive situations. I wonder if you chose to compete as a way to prove to yourself that you're a "good" drummer. In other words, if you had beaten the competition, would that mean you were a better drummer?

Most performing musicians have experienced at least one, if not many, auditions throughout the course of their careers. No way around it, this is a competitive situation. The band is looking for someone who will be the best fit. However, written or spoken descriptions of what an existing band is looking for are often vague and foggy. Obviously, don't show up for a formal wedding band audition in skateboarder kicks, ripped jeans, and a Bob Marley T-shirt. And if they give you several songs to learn, learn them! Drummer/percussionist Walfredo Reyes Jr. recently told me that you don't ever truly know what existing band members are looking for, even if their description of the perfect new drummer is clearly defined. For instance, how would you define feel? Wally's advice to me—as I was preparing for an audition myself—was simply to play my best and see what happens. That freed me from my anxieties of thinking, *What do they really want?*

I won't try to dissuade you from dropping your sticks and picking up a six-string. But before you do, please mull over what I've written, perform the exercises, and perhaps take a shot at another audition. Or christen yourself a bandleader and carve out a rehearsal space in your garage or basement, and then you can hold auditions for others. Best of luck!

You're Fired! (October 2010)

After I played in a band for ten months, the bandleader said to me before a recent rehearsal, "Sorry, it's just not working out. I have to ask you to leave." Then she asked me to pack up my gear. I feel really bad. I loved playing music with them, and I'm having a tough time getting over this. Any suggestions?

That's harsh. You're pissed, you're sad, you're hurt. A bandleader can phrase it however he or she wants, but the bottom line is always the same: "We don't want you."

It's important for you to express some of your initial feelings in meaningful but nondestructive ways. No wall punching or drinking yourself stupid and then going out and looking for a fight. If you want to punch something, beat up your pillow. Scream obscenities into it. Do push-ups until your arms feel like they're going to fall off. Play your drums—hard! All these behaviors are cathartic. Eventually the emotion of anger should subside. Physical activities will help you work the anger out of your system.

Sadness and hurt begin to creep in. Behind closed doors, shed some tears if you feel them beginning to flow. It's okay. Just let go. If the tears don't come, allow yourself to feel the sadness and hurt. Don't deny their presence.

Lastly, maybe talk with a good friend or one of your parents. Stay away from anyone who's preachy or would suggest an act of revenge. Choose someone who will just sit and listen to what you're feeling inside. Mental health professionals are also available. Do what feels right to you.

Now let's begin dealing with your loss—the loss of your band. There are five stages most people will work through, usually, but not always, in this order.

Stage 1: Denial

Man, you were blindsided, weren't you? It sounds like you never saw this coming. (Or did you?)

It's perfectly normal to deny anything happened to you. You might feel stunned or numb. But remind yourself that it's over. There's no going back. Unfortunately, there are no concrete, tangible reminders—like a cemetery headstone—to show you that your relationship with this band is dead. So, again, keep telling yourself that this is your reality.

Stage 2: Bargaining

In the bargaining stage, you may attempt to make deals, usually with God or the bandleader. "Please, God, I'll quit smoking if you can get me back in the band." Or, "Please, God, I'll go to church every Sunday for a year if you can just get me back in my old band." The hallmark of the bargaining phase is the word *please*.

Sometimes a drummer who's been involuntarily separated from his or her band will ask/bargain/beg the bandleader to be reinstated. I did this only once in my career. After I had a huge argument with a band-leader, he fired me. I apologized the next day, but his mind was made up. He repeated that my services were no longer needed. Ask to return if you feel compelled, and take responsibility for your part in why you were canned (if you do own a part). But never grovel.

If you want to try to get back in, it might be helpful if—over the phone—you ask your former bandleader what she meant by "It's just not working out." Maybe she'll remain vague, or maybe she'll go into specifics. If she does choose to explain her reasoning, be prepared for more ego bruising. What she tells you might hurt.

People are often vague with others for a number of reasons. Here are two that may fit your situation:

1. To protect you from further hurt. If she had said, "You suck as a drummer and we made a mistake hiring you," that could have provoked a mammoth emotional reaction from you.

2. To avoid drama. In being vague, your boss lessened a possible explosive reaction from you. You know yourself. Would you have gone off like a bottle rocket if she had said your drumming was lousy? Even though you had a ten-month run with them, she—or they, if it was a group decision—rejected you.

It's time to be totally honest with yourself. As I hinted above, maybe you knew this was coming but denied it. Your "sins" could include being chronically late for practice, using illicit substances, not being prepared, rushing or dragging tempos, playing the "wrong" feel…. There are a million and one reasons why. But if you denied or blew these things off, start fixing them now so you can avoid this pattern with your next band.

Stage 3: Depression/Sadness

We've already covered this above. However, many times when you think you've found closure with a particular emotion, it comes back like a thief in the night. Just keep expressing the emotions the best way you know how. Your goal is to reach a point where this painful experience becomes a memory without strong feelings.

Stage 4: Anger

After being fired, you may ask yourself, *Why me?* Well, you may know the reason, if it involved repeated unacceptable behaviors, or you may never know why this happened to you. If you feel as though your drumming was spot-on and you got along well with the band members, always showed up prepared, put on a good show, and so on, it may forever be a mystery why you were asked to leave. Some questions in life remain unanswered or are unanswerable.

Don't necessarily make your firing self-referential. By this, I mean don't assume it was your drumming that got you ousted. I've heard of excellent drummers getting bounced from their bands for the most ridiculous, nonsensical reasons. Humans don't always act in a logical fashion, and we as artists are often a wee bit wacky.

Also, always avoid any acts of revenge or retribution. You might fantasize about slashing your bandleader's tires, or punching her boyfriend in the face, or writing her phone number on the men's room wall. Getting back at someone usually feels good for about two minutes, and then you start to feel remorse. I understand that you got a raw deal, but two wrongs truly don't make a right. Plus, you might wind up with a lawsuit or a stint in the hoosegow.

Stage 5: Acceptance

This is not to be misinterpreted as "Yippee, I was fired!" Acceptance is more of a quiet acknowledgement that this very unpleasant episode in your drumming career occurred, and you've now moved past it.

In closing, if you had a hint that certain behaviors would eventually get you sacked, fix them. But if this event was truly a sucker punch, work the steps as outlined above, and eventually you'll get to the point where the incident is simply a memory without strong feelings.

Should you be unable to phase out feelings of sadness, depression, or anger—or should you have thoughts of hurting yourself or someone else because of this experience—please seek professional help. But I have a hunch that in time you'll be fine and will soon be performing with a new band. Always go where you're wanted. Good luck!

Accepting A Compliment (December 2010)

After playing drums in different types of bands, I think I've found the kind of music I really like and play well. I also found a group of musicians that I enjoy playing with. I'm getting a lot of compliments from the guys in my band and also from people in the audience during our set breaks. My problem is that I hear the words but don't really feel the compliments. Do you know what I mean?

You're probably not feeling the compliments because you really don't deserve them. Clubs are usually dimly lit. Are you sure the patrons aren't confusing you with the lead guitarist? I've heard he's excellent.

If my first statement knotted your stomach or maybe caused you to want to take a swing at me, good! That's the same visceral part of you we're going to work with so you can accept a compliment fully on an emotional level—not just hear it. (There's no truth in my leadoff statement; I only used it to provoke a strong gut reaction from you. Cool?)

Let's discuss compliments in a global sense and then focus on specifics.

Society's Take On Compliments

How many times have you witnessed—live, on TV, or in a movie—the following scenario? Most likely you've been both the giver and recipient of this type of compliment on many occasions. Pretend this exchange is between you and a coworker or a classmate.

Coworker/classmate: "I like your shirt."

You look down at your shirt, smirk, give it a tug, and respond, "This? It's cheap crap. I got it at the mall."

Your coworker/classmate raises his eyebrows, maybe looks a little wounded, says, "Oh...," and walks away.

This is a prime example of a classic lose/lose situation. Your coworker/classmate loses because now he or she feels foolish and awkward about giving you a compliment. You may have also, indirectly, sent the message that you think that person's taste in clothing is stupid.

You lose because you could have had a moment of feeling good. Obviously, you like something about the shirt, or you wouldn't have put it on that morning. For all we know, maybe it's your favorite shirt. You're not really being honest with yourself or your friend.

Why do we allow ourselves to lose out on these mini magic moments? Here are a couple of reasons:

1. By devaluing the compliment, you think it makes you look cool, sort of in the vein of, "Clothes? They ain't no big thang." It's as if you just blindly threw something on without any conscious thought. Most of us care about our appearance—to a lesser or greater extent. By brushing off

the compliment, you're trying to project a macho image. But it's probably not the real you.

2. By accepting the compliment, you think you'd appear haughty or arrogant. As in: "Yeah, I know I'm stylin'. I'm lookin' good." Society, for whatever reason, often fights to keep you from feeling good about yourself. You want evidence? Check out how many self-help, self-improvement, and self-esteem books, CDs, and seminars are currently offered in the United States. It's a multi-million-dollar business that attempts to offset society's often silent message to not feel good about what you're doing in your life.

Society also likes to gear its evaluations of our performances—whether they're on stage, at work, or in the classroom—toward the negative. You usually hear about the things that need improvement, without much focus on the tasks you're doing well. If you *do* hear a positive evaluation, it might be spoiled with a "but" statement.

For example, here's a comment a bandleader might make to a drummer: "Your single kick pedal work is fast and clean, *but* why can't you get a double pedal?" The problem is that the word *but* tends to negate everything good that comes before it. Substitute a different word and rephrase the request, and watch what happens.

Bandleader: "Your single kick pedal work is fast and clean, *and* we were wondering if you would consider experimenting with a double pedal to enhance the type of music we're playing."

With a statement like that you're more likely to accept the compliment on your single pedal playing and perhaps even be open to the possibility of trying out a double pedal.

Accepting A Compliment

Before you can learn to accept a compliment, you'll need to weed out the ones that are insincere. Learn to trust your gut, in conjunction with your ears. If the compliment is spoken in a smarmy voice, the speaker is either a jerk or jealous that you're on stage and he or she isn't. If the compliment doesn't ring true, you have every right to discount it.

When it comes time to receive an honest compliment, you have to first believe that you deserve the compliment. You said in your letter that you'd found music that you "really like and play well." That's fantastic! Continue to tell yourself that you play this type of music well.

When you first hear complimentary words from someone else, look the giver in the eye and offer your hand. Let the sincerity soak in. Allow yourself to feel good, even if it's only for a few milliseconds. It doesn't matter whether you're playing at a dumpy club to three patrons or at Madison Square Garden to thousands of devoted fans. It's still one human being taking the time and effort to tell you what a good job you've done and—perhaps—how your drumming affected him or her in a positive way.

Still holding eye contact, thank the person for giving the compliment. It may have taken a lot of courage for him or her to approach you. As crazy as it may seem, some people feel threatened by musicians, thinking they'll be mocked or blown off should they offer a compliment.

Accepting feedback in this manner creates a perfect win/win situation. You walk away feeling the emotion and sincerity of the compliment, while the one who spoke the kind words feels good knowing he or she gave you a gift. And that gift can only help to build self-confidence. Own it in the moment. This is your time.

The Drummer As Performer/Entertainer (February 2011)

I've been drumming with a band for the past five months, and the bandleader recently said I wasn't performing enough on stage. When I asked what she meant, she said my drumming was fine but I had no personality on stage. I told her that I was just concentrating, but she said my wooden appearance took away from the band's look. I have two questions: 1. Does a drummer have to be a performer/entertainer? 2. Can you help me save my job?

The answer to your first question depends largely on the context of the gig. That being said, keep one thing in mind: Your audience comes to *see* you perform just as much as, if not more than, to hear you play. Look at the outrageous ticket prices that big-name artists are getting for their concerts. With the amount you spend to see them on stage, you could buy their entire CD catalog. And why is that? It's because fans want the intimate experience of being in the same room as their favorite artists.

There's simply no comparison between hearing music through head-phones or on a car stereo versus being a part of the real-life concert experience, where the lights, the sound, and the band's performance come together as one.

Let's further examine a gig's context as being a factor in whether drummers specifically need to be performers/entertainers, using three legendary players as examples: Ringo Starr, Charlie Watts, and Keith Moon.

In their heyday, the Beatles wore matching outfits and haircuts to immediately identify themselves as members of the band. In addition, each Beatle had his own persona. Ringo Starr would smile, flip his mop-top hairdo around while playing fills, and tilt his head to let his long hair flop when hitting a song-ending cymbal crash. Was his showmanship outrageous? Of course not. But Ringo's stage appearance, when combined with his drumming, absolutely constituted showmanship.

Now let's look at Charlie Watts of the Rolling Stones. When Watts plays on his no-frills four-piece kit, his expression is the quintessential poker face—one that leaves spectators wondering whether he's deep in thought, tranquil, reserved, or perhaps even bored. He really doesn't give much away beyond the occasional grin. Watts, however, is sharing the stage with Mick Jagger and Keith Richards, two individuals who have defined the term *rock star*, so there's little need for Charlie to do anything other than play his kit.

On the opposite end of the spectrum, the Who's Keith Moon had an innocent choirboy look but bashed his drums like a wild man. The Who's live show was a spectacle, and singer Roger Daltrey, guitarist Pete Townshend, and Moon all placed a high priority on showmanship. The band's bassist, John Entwistle, was the lone holdout.

As you can see from these examples, context is key when it comes to whether or not a drummer *has* to be a showman. Your band and your role within it will help you determine the appropriate context.

On to your second question: Can I help you save your job? Yes! Start by asking your bandleader what specifically she wants you to do in terms of increasing your performance quotient. I'm guessing she has an image in mind of what she expects. If she does detail her specific wants, the question you then have to answer is: Am I willing to meet her expectations?

If she's too vague in her descriptions or wants you to invent your own stage persona, here are a few places to start.

1. Facial expressions. For starters, smile! Smile at your bandmates and especially at the audience. Remember, they've come to the club to be entertained. Show them you're having a good time, and they will mirror your behavior. If the music is heavier, experiment with some more intense expressions. Match what you put on your face with the feel of the song. You can also try moving your head in time to the music. (Often, a performer's facial expressions are an involuntary response to the emotions evoked by the music. If you're playing with an expressionless look, you may want to spend time reconnecting with the core feelings of the music and allow them to pour out of you while performing.)

2. Flash. For more extreme showmanship, learn to twirl your sticks. Perhaps this routine is a bit overdone, but it still seems to be a crowd pleaser when used in the appropriate context. There are plenty of DVDs, CDs, and books on the topic.

3. Movement. On certain songs, dramatize your movements. For example, if you kick off a song with a flam, raise your arms high over your head and make it look like the most impassioned drum part you've ever performed in your life. I'm not asking you to change your overall technique but rather to create a mixed bag of stage-presence ideas and then pull stuff out when appropriate. Just be sure to use them sparingly, so your moves don't become predictable. The element of surprise can be quite effective.

4. End with a bang. Finish your songs with dramatic flair. If you usually rely on simple cymbal crashes or flams to close out a tune, prep your bandmates that you're going to go for something different. Try long cymbal swells, or play a short solo. The point is to execute something totally unexpected (to the crowd, not to your band).

5. Image. Try changing up what you wear for your performances. A simple black T-shirt always works on stage, but it can be a bit boring if you're trying to boost the visual impact. A slick-looking vest, a collared shirt, or a cool hat can do a lot to bump up your appearance.

There's always the possibility that nothing you do will make your bandleader satisfied with your stage presence. It can be a bummer, but perhaps it's time to move on, which leads to one last option: Don't change anything. I know you want to keep this gig, but at what cost? If you're content with the way you're performing, there are other bands out there that I'm guessing would gladly take you just as you are—no changes required.

My Dad's Kit (April 2011)

I'm sixteen years old and have been playing drums for about five months. When I started playing, my dad gave me his old kit and was very excited about me following in his footsteps. The problem is, I really don't like his drums. They're old and have been stored in the basement for years. The white finish has yellowed, and there's rust on the chrome. Plus it's only a four-piece kit. I don't want to hurt his feelings, but I really want a new kit in a fade finish with a bunch of toms, maybe even two bass drums. I'm in a band, but we haven't played out yet. When that time comes, I can't imagine playing my first gig with my dad's old, beat-up drums. What do I do?

Let me preface my response by saying that I can only illuminate different choices, or possible solutions, that you haven't yet considered. I can't tell you what to do. Ultimately, *you* will need to make the decisions regarding your dilemma.

First, let's look at your concern about the number of drums on your kit. Every Saturday night, at approximately 11:34 P.M., after a cast member shouts out, "Live from New York, it's Saturday night!" Shawn Pelton's job as the house drummer on *Saturday Night Live* is to amp up the live and TV audience. He plays with his whole being—his mind, his heart, his hands, and his feet—and he does so on a four-piece kit. That's all he needs to get the job done...and done *well*.

Shawn is in good company too. Dave Grohl (Nirvana, Foo Fighters), Josh Freese (studio ace), Questlove (the Roots), Abe Laboriel Jr. (Paul McCartney), Steve Jordan (R&B/pop drummer extraordinaire), Charlie Watts (the Rolling Stones), Stanton Moore (Galactic), Dominic Howard (Muse), Justin Foley (Killswitch Engage)—the list goes on and on—all choose to play small kits. Why? Because what really matters is not the number of drums you play, but *how* you play the drums you have.

A big kit with a gorgeous finish always catches my eye when I see one in an ad or stroll into a music store. Major drum companies spend big bucks on photography to make their products look absolutely irresistible. When Zak Starkey played his double bass rig at the 2010 Super Bowl, he looked and sounded awesome. Big kits undeniably have their place in music. But remember that you haven't even played your first gig yet.

At sixteen, you may actually have difficulty in being allowed to perform at venues that serve alcohol. Let's assume, though, that you are able to play at a nightclub, bar, or roadhouse. You'll be surprised by what constitutes a "stage" at some of these venues. A miniscule swatch of carpeting in a far-off corner may be the only space you have to set up your drums. A club owner's job is to hear the sweet ring of his cash register. The more space he allots for a band, the fewer patrons he can cram into his club. If you wind up playing house parties, youth centers, or maybe at your high school, you'll probably encounter similar space issues, unless you're lucky enough to score the stage in the school's auditorium.

I would never dissuade you from purchasing that tobacco-fade-finish kit with two kicks and a slew of toms, but unless you have an extended-body cargo van, have you considered how you're going to cart around your massive arsenal?

Consider these alternatives to rushing out and buying an enormous kit:

1. Chrome can be cleaned and rust can be removed. Google "rust removers." I use Espirit D-Ruster, which is nontoxic and environmentally safe.

2. Rims/hoops and other hardware can be replaced if the rust is too thick.

3. You can recover your four-piece kit. There are ads in the back of *Modern Drummer* that offer a wealth of new and dazzling finishes. You can have your set professionally recovered, or you can do it yourself. If you decide to try it yourself, I recommend the DVD *Guerrilla Drum Making*.

4. You can use a double pedal instead of two bass drums.

Your dad gifted you his drums, a possession that at one point in his life was probably very important to him. That's an act of love. The fact that you don't want to hurt his feelings suggests that you two have a good relationship. The one statement you made that has me a little uncomfortable is about your dad's excitement over your "following in his footsteps." You've been playing for only five months. It's hard to predict whether you'll stick with it. If you decide to quit, will that dash whatever expectations he may have?

If you decide to buy a big kit and use that instead of his vintage set, I'm guessing that your dad might be a little hurt. It's a rejection of sorts, but perhaps he'll realize that you and he are bound to have different tastes in music, drums, and drummers. Good luck!

Band Versus Solo (June 2011)

I always wanted to play drums, so I bought a cheap set at a garage sale. When I come home from school, I go into my basement and pound away. I have fun playing along to CDs, which helps me unwind after a stressful day.

I'm a high school senior and a member of a local drama club. Rehearsals for a play will be starting soon, and I'm also active in my church. Here's my problem. My church has live music. The regular drummer got sick recently, and my minister asked if I could be the new drummer. Several of my friends also keep asking me to start a band with them. I have no motivation to be in a band, and I don't feel qualified to play in church. One of my friends gave me a copy of Modern Drummer *in hopes that it would inspire me to start rehearsing with him. That's how I came across your column. Can you offer any advice?*

I'm sorry, but I can't help you—because you really don't have a problem. You're playing your drums exactly the way you desire. You're using the drumkit like someone else might use a treadmill or a set of free weights. As you clearly stated, "I have fun playing along to CDs, which helps me unwind after a stressful day."

Humans vacillate between having a need for solitude and a need for communion. Spending time alone with your drums fulfills your need for a little escape from the world. The drama club and your church activities give you the camaraderie and connections that can be had only by being with other people. From your letter, it seems as if you've established a nice balance of the two.

The only problem I see in your situations is with friends who are pestering you to take your relationship with the drums to a different level. Have your friends who are bugging you to start a band ever been in any sort of musical ensemble before? (And I'm not talking about school-sponsored groups, where many, if not all, of the managerial details have been taken care of by school personnel.) Starting and maintaining a band takes a tremendous amount of work. Let's use your drama club as an analogy. Members of the club and its advisor decide which play you're going to perform. Then you hold auditions, followed by weeks, or even months, of rehearsals. Then you have a series of performances.

If your friends keep insisting that you form a band together, try asking them a few of these questions:

1. Where will we rehearse if not in my basement, and how often?
2. Who chooses the songs?
3. When we have enough songs to play out, who will book shows for the band?
4. Where will we play?
5. Does anyone have a PA? If not, how will we go about purchasing one?
6. Do we—or our parents—have a vehicle large enough to carry our equipment to shows?

If your friends are still intent on recruiting you, simply look them straight in the eyes and say, "I have no interest or time to do this." That should get your point across.

Lastly, I'm assuming your minister accepted your refusal to be the church's new drummer. If he or she pushes the issue, push back (gently) by highlighting the fact that you really don't have any interest in playing drums publicly. Simply continue to enjoy drumming as a solo hobby that offers escapism and stress relief. (Remember to wear ear protection!) And don't ever be afraid to say no. It's your life, and how you choose to spend your free time is ultimately your choice.

Drinking, Drugging, and Drumming (August 2011)

I often have a couple drinks before gigs, including some afternoon wedding receptions. I do this just to loosen up and take the edge off. My wife says I'm an alcoholic because I'm drinking during the day. I never drink to the point of being falling-down drunk, and our bandleader hasn't seemed to notice any problem with my playing. What's your take on this?

On his album *Life Is Messy*, country artist Rodney Crowell sings a song called "It's Not For Me To Judge." That's where I'm at with your situation. Realize, though, that if your wife drags you to an alcoholism counselor, the counselor will say that you're engaging in what the substance abuse treatment field calls relief drinking. By drinking, you're achieving relief from anxiety.

As drummers we're encouraged to stay loose and relaxed when we play. An uptight drummer's playing often sounds stiff, tension in the body can have adverse effects on time feel, and the audience doesn't want to look at a musician who's a bundle of nerves. Alcohol is a drug that reliably induces relaxation. There are certainly other ways to achieve relaxation, but alcohol and other drugs—specifically minor tranquilizers like Xanax and Valium—are reliable substances for providing that feeling you desire.

Now, before you write in accusing me of promoting the use of alcohol and/or other drugs, realize that I'm simply explaining why humans use specific substances: The desired effect tends to be predicable and reliable should we choose to take the drug.

With you, there's a strong association between performing and lowering your anxiety with alcohol. Chugging a few drinks by yourself before a gig has no social benefit, like what you would experience drinking a beer or two at the end of the night with your bandmates. There's a big difference between the two situations.

There's a model for understanding alcohol and drug use, called "medicating for feelings," that appears to fit your particular case.

Let's look at another drug that musicians may be prone to use: cocaine. Let's pretend that your band makes the leap from small clubs to concert venues. You've hit the big time! There's no book or college course to prepare you for this. You feel a mixture of excitement and, perhaps, outright fear. If you choose to deal with the fear by using a drug, you'll either want to go "up" or "down." If you're feeling inadequate, ill prepared, or just plain terrified to face a throng of screaming fans before a performance, you may be drawn to a drug that induces feelings of competence, confidence, power, and control. Snorting powder cocaine or smoking crack just before the gig will give you those feelings. (Again, I'm not promoting the use of cocaine; I'm just explaining why, and in which context, an individual may choose to use the drug.)

The flip side is to choose to deal with your anxiety by using some sort of sedative. In this situation you're looking to bring the excitement level down. In 1973, while playing a concert at the Cow Palace in California, the Who's Keith Moon collapsed onto his kit after supposedly taking animal tranquilizers. I'm guessing he wanted to quell some of the anxiety related to the pandemonium of this particular show.

After becoming sober, Ringo Starr admitted to not remembering many of the concerts at the huge venues where the Beatles had played. In the drug and alcohol treatment field, this state of not remembering is called a blackout.

Okay, so now that I've explained the models, I have a few questions for you. First, what feelings are you medicating for? Your relationship with alcohol is an important one, since you have to go to a liquor store to buy booze before your gigs. That's a commitment that you *choose* to make.

Your relationship with alcohol also has a specific association: Drink, and then play. Can you perform in public without having alcohol in your system? What would happen if you didn't have access to alcohol before playing a gig? Do you fear that your hands and feet wouldn't move?

I remember a drummer stating in an interview something to the effect that after he quit drinking he had to relearn how to do everyday tasks without alcohol. It's similar to when someone quits smoking cigarettes. When you were a smoker, your whole day was filled with associations. Wake up, light up. Finish breakfast, fire up a smoke. Turn the key in your car's ignition, reach for your lighter. Depending on how many packs a former smoker smoked, there could have been up to eighty associations per day.

You asked for my take on your situation, and there you have it. No judging, no preaching, just an explanation as to why someone might consume a mood-altering chemical, followed by some hard questions that you need to ask yourself. At one point in my counseling career, I worked at an inpatient drug rehab. The walls were covered with signs displaying slogans and catchphrases. There was one in particular—with a decidedly non–Alcoholics Anonymous philosophy—that will always stay with me. It was handwritten and encased in a simple black frame. It read: "Habits are at first cobwebs…then cables."

Chapter 9: One-Shots

T o conclude our journey, I want to present a series of quick solutions to various drumming-related issues that you may experience at some point in your musical career. Sometimes the best solutions are the simplest.

"I feel like I have to hit harder to convey energy and excitement."
Where is that written? Try using facial expressions instead. Buddy Rich was a master at conveying emotional excitement with his face. There's an old expression regarding performance: "Take something easy and make it look hard; take something hard and make it look easy."

"I'm afraid to take risks when playing in public. My drumming on stage is very safe."
If you're real careful, no harm or good will ever come to you.

"I rush the first few songs of a set."
Try some relaxation exercises. It's all about controlling the flow of adrenaline. Then again, listen to some of the early Police albums. Stewart Copeland rushed many of the songs, but that didn't keep him from becoming one of the most influential drummers of all time.

"I have difficulty playing on other drummers' kits at open mics."
Doesn't everyone? I'd be surprised if you felt totally comfortable sitting on a stool that's too low, playing cymbals that are too high, or hitting a snare that's tuned so loosely that the head is practically flapping. It's like driving somebody else's car. As much as you adjust the mirrors and seats, you never feel a hundred percent comfortable. Just accept that it's going to be a little different, and focus your attention on making music.

"I let a mistake or two ruin my gig."
You're mentally frozen in time. You've physically moved past your mistakes, but you just don't realize it. Time moves forward, not backward, and it never stands still. Don't concern yourself with the audience catch-

ing your mistake. There's a chance many of them saw it, but if they did they probably didn't care. Take responsibility for your perception of the gig. You can focus on the ninety-nine percent of the gig that went well and feel good about it, or you can obsess about the one percent of the time when you goofed up. It's your choice.

"I'm stuck in my head when performing."
I hope you're not trying to solve some complex algebraic formulas or attempting to figure out the meaning of life. Try this. Focus, momentarily, on something outside yourself. Choose something that isn't going to provoke a lot of thought. Focus on someone at the bar, or focus on the tawdry purple velvet curtains the owner has hung over the windows. Or, better yet, find a face in the crowd that's smiling and really digging your music. Or send a smile out to a bandmate, a patron, or the bartender. When you put one of these strategies to work, you're out of your head and your body is free to play the songs.

"Why do I sound totally different on recordings from the way I thought I would?"
Because studio mics hear everything!

When a novelist pens a book, he or she hopes the reader doesn't notice sloppy writing, boring stories, weak plots, cardboard characters, and so on. So while proofreading a draft, the author—consciously or unconsciously—skips or skims over these troubling parts. It's the same thing when you play and listen to yourself in a live performance setting. You skip or skim the parts that are shaky, and you pretend that no one will notice. (It's very likely that no one will.) But unless your recording engineer is doing something unusual, those mics are capturing the truth.

"I feel embarrassed when my band plays a gig and I have to use my beat-up drumkit, especially if we're the opening act for a group whose drummer has top-of-the-line equipment."
Who cares what your kit looks like? How do you *sound*? That's the most important thing. Plus, entry-level drums often sound better if you simply upgrade the heads and learn how to tune them properly. Stop worrying

about the appearance of your kit, and focus on its sound and the music you're making.

"I always kill it when I audition for bands, but the gig always goes to some bozo who I know isn't as good as me. How come?"
You have an arrogant attitude, you're angry, and you probably exude a know-it-all persona at these auditions. Think about it: Would *you* want to hire someone who puts out that kind of vibe? Assertiveness and confidence are great traits to have in life, but arrogance usually turns people off. Be confident and prepared, but also be friendly. And don't let the bitterness of all the jobs you didn't get affect how you act at your next audition. If you're as skilled a player as you believe, you'll increase your chances of landing the gig if you work on being a friendlier person.

"I don't want to learn to read music because it'll stifle my creativity."
Reading music stifles creativity? How do you know that to be true? That's like saying, "I refuse to listen to any other drummers and will avoid any type of instructional materials because it might taint my own intrinsic ability to create." Learning to read music will help make you a well-rounded and more employable musician. For example, what do you think will happen if a bandleader hands you a chart during an audition and you can't play it? It doesn't matter how many chops you have if you can't execute the task at hand. You simply won't get the gig.

Plus, having the ability to read music allows you to discover and explore musical ideas that might be a bit beyond your current physical and conceptual skill level on the drums. Isn't that what creativity is all about—finding something new?

"I've always been faithful in keeping with a practice routine, dedicating as much time as possible to my drumming and music. But now that I have a full-time job I'm often too exhausted in the evening to get behind the drums. I've noticed that my technique is starting to suffer a bit. How do I get back in the zone?"
Get your butt off the couch, toss the Twinkies, and make a public commitment (to your girlfriend, wife, parents, etc.) that you're going to play your drums every day after work for a specific period of time, at least

three times a week. You need to change up your routine when you get home from work. Try going directly to your kit—without thinking—to jam out. Unless you're running a jackhammer all day, your exhaustion is of the mental variety, and there's nothing more cathartic and energizing than letting loose for a bit on the drums.

Also, stop calling it "practice," which could have strong associations with drudgery and rote repetition. Make mental movies where you see yourself playing at your finest and enjoying the play/practice session (pleasure-based motivation). Or make mind movies where you're flopped on the couch, balancing a bag of chips on a big beer belly, while your once-beautiful drums start to decay with rust in your basement (pain-based motivation).

"We're having a difficult time building a fan base for our band."
For an extreme effect, take off some of your clothes. Not all of them, but enough to make a difference. The Red Hot Chili Peppers have been known to rock out nearly naked with just a white athletic sock covering their private parts. Also, remember when Gwen Stefani of No Doubt used to wear cutoff shirts so she could expose her perfectly sculpted abs, and drummer Adrian Young wore nothing but a thong in performance?

And that's the key word: *performance*. If the audience only wants to hear music, they'll stay home and listen to a CD. The visual aspect of a live performance is essential. If you're going to stare down at your shoes all night, wondering if your pedal is still attached to your kick drum hoop, maybe you're better off being a studio drummer, where it's just you and the recording engineer.

"I think I'm falling in love with the singer in my band. Whenever we practice or play a gig, I can't keep my mind on my drumming."
What's more important to you, the possibility of having a relationship with your singer or continuing to play with this band? Has your singer expressed any feelings of wanting more than a professional relationship with you? Rock music can be inherently sexual, but you may be making a huge mistake in thinking that when your singer is bustin' a move on

stage, it's for you. Truth is, he or she might just be an excellent entertainer and is simply playing to the audience.

Maybe if the two of you do get together, it'll work out and the band will be able to absorb this new relationship. I'd be remiss, though, if I didn't speculate that if you change the dynamic between you and the rest of your bandmates, unpleasant emotions (jealousy, competitiveness, awkwardness, anger, sadness, etc.) could begin to come forth. Either way, don't let your infatuation with your singer cause your drumming to suffer, or else you may soon find yourself looking for a new gig instead of a new dance partner.